Understanding
YOUR Dog

Understanding
YOUR Dog

NEW
HOLLAND

Dr Elsa Flint

First published in 2003 by
New Holland Publishers
London • Cape Town • Sydney • Auckland
www.newhollandpublishers.com

86 EDGWARE ROAD
LONDON W2 2EA
UNITED KINGDOM

14 AQUATIC DRIVE
FRENCHS FOREST, NSW 2086
AUSTRALIA

80 MCKENZIE STREET
CAPE TOWN 8001
SOUTH AFRICA

218 LAKE ROAD
NORTHCOTE, AUCKLAND
NEW ZEALAND

ISBN 1 84330 449 X (HB), 1 84330 450 3 (PB)

Publisher: Mariëlle Renssen
Publishing managers: Claudia Dos Santos, Simon Pooley
Commissioning editor: Alfred LeMaitre
Studio manager: Richard MacArthur
Editor: Katja Splettstoesser
Designer: Christelle Marais
Illustrator: Steven Felmore
Picture researcher: Karla Kik
Proofreader/Indexer: Leizel Brown
Production: Myrna Collins
Consultant: Bas Hagreis BVSc(Hons) MRCVS

Reproduction by Hirt & Carter (Cape) Pty Ltd
Printed and bound in Singapore by Tien Wah Press (Pte) Ltd

2 4 6 8 10 9 7 5 3 1

Right *Family life is all the more enriched by our canine companions as
they integrate themselves effortlessly into our daily routines, sharing in
our social, leisure and household activities.*

Contents

A Dog in the Family

For most people a dog represents companionship, and indeed it makes a great companion. Unfortunately many people have unrealistic expectations when they make the decision to own a dog. Their reasons are many and varied, some are valid and others are not. Dogs are not substitute human beings. They have their own needs and their own psyche. The relationship between dog and owner is a two-way street and it is important that we, as owners, try to understand the world from our dog's point of view. Doing so should help avoid the development of some behavioural problems commonly found in canines, and will also help owners recognize problems as they arise and understand how to deal with them.

Left *Making an effort to understand your dog — and carefully managing it — will make having a pet so much more rewarding for you.*

Wanted: *Single human male seeks canine companion. Must be loyal, faithful, enjoy walks in the park, days at the beach, rides in the car, soccer, tennis and possibly sailing. Must be able to cope alone at home if owner has to work in dog-unfriendly situations. Should be happy to defend the property from unwanted intruders but must not bite friends...*

Wanted: *Friendly, cute, cuddly canine to share family life with two adults and three children aged between three and seven years. Must be house-trained, must not dig, bark, jump up, or chew household or garden items. Must be prepared to be squeezed, poked, dressed up and dragged around by exuberant children without complaining. Must be happy with one walk daily and should not complain if this is forgotten due to family commitments...*

If a dog were to advertise for an owner, it might go something like this:

Wanted: *Dependable, small human 'pack'. Must work together to defend territory and should avoid independent wanderings. Must enjoy daily investigation of the home, and respect the need to mark territory. Den should be warm and dry with a soft sleeping area and should be situated near a plentiful food supply. Ground should be easy to dig for bone-burying purposes. Younger 'pack' members should be well disciplined.*

A dog's needs and expectations are quite simple: a stable, secure environment, companionship with a clearly defined pack hierarchy, clearly delineated territory, plentiful food and water, shelter and access to an interesting home range. A human's needs and expectations of its dog are often quite different. The dog is expected to behave like a human child in some instances and like a responsible human adult in others. It is all too often expected to cope in today's busy, erratic and unstable households, and is fitted into family life when time allows. It is this mismatch of needs and expectations that leads to many perceived problem dog behaviours, resulting in unhappy dogs and owners.

Keeping a dog in today's society is about balancing the needs of dog and owner. This can be more difficult than it sounds. Unfortunately, quality dogs are euthanased or dumped in animal shelters every day due to behavioural problems. Of course there are dogs that are neurologically abnormal and which show extreme and unusual behavioural patterns as a result. In many cases, however, problem behaviours have arisen simply as a result of misunderstandings between dog and owner.

Left *To forge a healthy relationship with your dog, make sure you don't treat it like a doll or a surrogate child.*

SO WHO SHOULD OWN A DOG?

Before you buy a dog, the main factors to consider include: available space for the dog, the time and costs involved in animal ownership, the age of your children and the stability of your life for the next 10 to 15 years.

SPACE

To own a dog you ideally need an outdoor area sized 125m² (150 sq yd) for a small dog and 250m² (299 sq yd) for a medium to large dog. The actual area needed may also vary according to the activity level of the dog. You will not find it easy to accommodate a German Short-haired Pointer or Border Collie if you have a tiny garden. The space should also, preferably, not be perfectly landscaped and pristine.

Above *Confining a large or highly active dog to a tiny apartment compromises its physical and mental wellbeing.*

There has to be room for the dog to run and play, and defecate well away from the immediate living area. However, having said that, remember that no matter how big the garden is, your dog will still need to go out for walks both for physical and mental wellbeing. For a dog, going for a walk beyond the property is like a human reading the paper or watching the news. It receives information about other dogs and animals that have passed by, through scent and, sometimes, visual markers. It is also an opportunity for social contact and play with other dogs.

TIME

Puppies are very time-consuming, especially during the first three months with the family. To house-train one successfully, you need to be with the puppy almost all the time (see pp34–36). You can leave it for two hours in a confined sleeping area if it has been out to relieve itself first, but you cannot expect a young puppy (less than four months of age) to wait much longer before needing to defecate again. You need to be vigilant to help it.

As an adult, the dog should, preferably, not be alone for more than four hours daily. So unless you are home most of the time, have the option to take the dog to work with you or have a daytime dogsitter, it is unfair to consider taking on a dog.

You will also need time and energy to walk the dog, preferably, twice daily for at least 30 minutes; patience and willingness to take the dog to puppy school and/or dog training; and the commitment to follow through on this with back-up training at home.

Right *Quality pet foods can be relatively expensive, so ensure your budget covers the necessary monthly cost.*
Below *Owning a dog is a major responsibility particularly with regards to setting aside sufficient time to exercise it.*

Above *Parents should always supervise the interaction between the family dog and a baby.*

COSTS

Consider the ongoing costs of feeding, registration fees, veterinary fees, collars and leads, and training courses. Ask friends who own dogs what their costs amount to; this will give you some idea of what to expect.

THE FUTURE

If you are in a stable job and you are unlikely to receive a posting abroad in the near future, you can probably provide the security a dog needs.

If you are a young person considering university in one or two years, it is unwise to convince the family to allow you to take on a dog only to leave it for them to take care of when you move away or into a city flat. Dogs become very attached to their owners and often become traumatized when forcibly separated from them.

CHILDREN

If you have children, it is easier — and advisable — to wait until your youngest child is at least five, preferably seven years old, before getting a puppy. This recommendation is given due to the fact that young children and puppies do not interact well together and adult dogs need an adjustment period when a new baby arrives in a household.

Most people have a romantic picture in their mind of dogs and children romping through the grass together. Yes, this type of relationship does exist, and it can be formed through persistent training, but a lot of groundwork is necessary to achieve this ideal.

Dogs, unfortunately do not automatically look after babies, and are prone to seriously hurting children as a result of grave misinterpretations of infant behaviour.

SELECTING THE RIGHT BREED

Having decided that the time is appropriate for you to take on a dog, see your veterinary surgeon to discuss which breeds you should consider. Many practices offer pre-pet counselling and they are in a good position to advise on breed traits, although these traits can only be used as an indicator and are not a guarantee of future behaviour.

Taking this into account, if you have an adolescent family with a high physical activity level or you are a keen jogger, you may enjoy a dog with a high energy level such as a Jack Russell Terrier, a Dalmatian, or a German Short-

Above *If you are a keen jogger, and in the process of selecting a dog, choose a breed with a high activity level.*

haired Pointer. If you are more sedentary, however, a Bichon Frise would be more appropriate.

Some breeds have a stronger tendency to guard than others – some will retrieve naturally, while others tend to be less interested in games and duties (see pp42–43). Give some thought to your expectations of a dog and select a breed that is suited to your lifestyle and temperament.

You may decide to choose one of the many cross-bred puppies in need of a home. You cannot predict their personalities so easily, but they are often delightful pets.

Note that all puppies, no matter what breed, will go through difficult phases. They will chew things, mouth and nip at people, and jump up in excitement. They may dig holes in the garden, knock things over during play, grab washing off the line and generally try your patience. With training, these behaviours will be overcome and most dogs will be delightful companions by 18 months of age.

CHOOSING YOUR PUPPY

Having decided on a breed or type of dog that you'd like, contact a kennel club for a list of reputable breeders. Visit those that have available litters and make a point of interacting with the puppies.

Try to meet the parents. If they are both relaxed and friendly, there is a good chance their offspring will have a similar temperament. Visit the litter several times at weekly intervals while the puppies are between six and nine weeks of age, and then select the puppy that most appeals to you.

Right *Although it is not easy to predict their personalities, puppies that exhibit a playful willingness to interact often make the best pets for first-time dog owners.*
Below *If you are choosing a puppy from a litter, be sure to visit the parents regularly while the puppies are between six and nine weeks of age, before deciding which one you would like to take home.*

It is difficult to assess a puppy's future temperament because it changes almost weekly. Some breeders will talk about temperament testing and will offer to select a puppy for you, based on a series of tests. This, unfortunately, is of little value.

As a first-time owner, it is wise to avoid a puppy that is pushy or exceptionally retiring. Look simply for a playful willingness to interact and then go with your instinct and choose the one you like the most.

If you are selecting a dog from an animal shelter, spend some time watching the dogs that are available and avoid those exhibiting extreme forms of behaviour. It is easy to feel sorry for the puppy that hides in the corner, thinking it may have been mistreated and will improve with a loving owner. You may be right, but you might also be selecting a genetically dysfunctional animal which you may find difficult to cope with once it has settled into your home (see p20).

If you respond when the puppy cries during the first night or two, it will cry every night. If you ignore the behaviour it will sleep through after the first two or three nights. Ensure the puppy is taken out to defecate last thing at night (23:00) and first thing in the morning (06:00). After four to five months of age they can manage to hold on a little longer, perhaps from 22:00 to 07:00.

The puppy will need to be fed four meals daily until it is three months old, then three meals daily until six months old, then twice daily. It will need to be taken outside to defecate before and after feeding, 10 minutes into a play session and whenever it starts to wander aimlessly and

Left *Every puppy should be provided with its own secure sleeping area, a comfortable bed and a selection of toys. If you are opting for crate training (see p36), a playpen or large travelling cage can be used in this designated area.*
Below *Puppies must be taken out regularly to defecate.*

PUPPY PARENTING

Make an effort to learn as much as possible about normal dog behaviour so that you know what to expect before getting a puppy. Once you have selected one you will probably bring it home between nine and 12 weeks. Note that your puppy's vaccinations must be given between six and 12 weeks. Check with your veterinary surgeon as to the exact requirements in your area.

Remember to never leave it with free access to all the rooms of the house; it should be in view at all times. Be consistent with your puppy. Have a bed-area ready and once you've chosen this spot, stick to your decision. Provide a large stuffed toy for your puppy to cuddle up to and a luke-warm hot-water bottle beneath its bedding.

If you want the puppy to sleep in your bedroom as an adult then allow it to do so as a puppy but don't start off feeling sorry for the puppy and then change your mind when the dog gets too big or unruly. The puppy will not understand your change of heart and will subsequently refuse to sleep elsewhere.

sniff. Go out with the puppy, wait until it has obliged and praise it for doing so.

If your puppy makes a mistake inside the house and you see it has just happened, do not yell; just soak up or pick up the mistake, take it outside and praise the puppy next to the evidence. This reinforces the right place for urine and faeces. If the mistake happened when you were out of sight and you find it without the puppy near, simply clean it up and forget about addressing the issue.

Puppies love to play and this is crucial for their development. How you play with them is important. Do not roughhouse with them, pushing them about with your hands. This encourages nipping and, while it seems funny in a tiny puppy, it is not funny in a 20kg (45lb) dog. Play instead with toys; tug toys, in particular, are fine. Squeaky toys and balls are always popular. Remember, most importantly, to discourage children from playing chasing games with puppies as this usually ends in tears.

Enrol your animal in puppy preschool as soon as you can. Through this, puppies learn to interact with other dogs and begin early obedience training. Practise the training protocols at home daily; you will be amazed at how quickly your puppy will learn.

Your puppy's window of opportunity for effective socialization closes between 14 and 15 weeks of age, and although it may not have yet received its final vaccination at 12 weeks, try if possible to introduce it to vaccinated companion dogs prior to this.

After it has been vaccinated take it for short car rides to fun destinations and introduce it to parks, outdoor cafés and beaches.

SETTING GUIDELINES

Dogs are group-living animals, and harmonious living within the group is achieved by establishing a hierarchy.

Your dog relates to the family in the same way as it would to a group of dogs and it needs to know where it stands in the hierarchy of the household. Be clear and consistent with your expectations. You are in control.

Above *To ensure a manageable dog, practise training it regularly from a young age both indoors and out in the open.*

If you are happy for the puppy to sit on the sofa, that's fine but it should be at your invitation. Ask the puppy to sit on the floor first, then allow it to jump onto the sofa. On occasion refuse to allow the privilege and ask the puppy to lie on the floor instead where you have a beanbag or alternative comfortable bedding.

You must be the one with priority access to favoured areas and the puppy should not be allowed to take over these areas. If it does, it may begin to dominate the family and the result is a dog that growls and nips when you ask it to get down from the chair or when you step over it or inadvertently lean on it (see p58).

While getting things right during puppyhood can help prevent the development of many problem behaviours in adult dogs, it is by no means the only answer. Behaviour is influenced by many different factors.

Behavioural Influences

Your dog's behaviour is the result of a number of linked factors including its genetic make-up, physiological state – such as hormones, old age and illness – past experiences and its environment. By understanding these factors and how they influence your dog's interaction with you and the world around it, you will find you are able to control and even possibly change some of its negative behaviour for the better. Many behavioural problems arise from lack of understanding and consequent miscommunication between dog and owner. Normal behaviour may become problem behaviour if a dog is handled incorrectly. Of course there are also behavioural patterns that arise from neurological abnormalities. Many of these can be modified and managed with the help of an animal behaviourist.

Left *Introducing your dog to stimulating environments will prevent boredom and enable it to react calmly to novel stimuli.*

GENES

Why does your dog bark and growl at intruders, enjoy digging, wag its tail, urinate on upright objects, sniff the ground, kick out with its hind feet after passing urine? Why does it roll in rotting fish and chase cats? The answers: because as a dog, it has become genetically pro-grammed to behave in certain typical ways.

As with any gene pool, it is possible to select for or against some behavioural traits, and this accounts for certain typical breed characteristics (see pp42–43). For example, terriers tend to bark more frequently and chase small furry animals with less provocation than some other breeds; Basset Hounds and Bloodhounds, on the other hand, follow scent, while Greyhounds are highly motivated to chase anything that runs.

Furthermore, Border Collies have a natural tendency to herd and stare intently at stock or sheep intimidating them into moving in a particular direction, a behavioural trait known as 'giving eye'.

Above *At a glance, all these puppies appear to have good physical traits but determining an individual animal's temperament requires regular visits to the litter.*

Many problems arise, however, when a breeder selects animals for the replication of physical traits that are desirable for the show-ring, but overlooks their temperaments. An example of such a mismatch is where an owner seeks a dog with a bold upright carriage, a physical trait most often linked to dominance aggression. In this case, the dog as well as its puppies could, at some stage, exhibit dominance aggression, a behavioural trait in which it shows excessive and often unprovoked aggression towards its unsuspecting owner.

This type of dog can be extremely dangerous around people. Constant selection, therefore, of breeds with particular physical traits associated with dominance aggression results in an unbalanced animal.

THE BRAIN

A dog's brain is the control centre for its body and, as such, is responsible for monitoring its behaviour. The main part of the brain influencing behaviour is the limbic system which features the brain stem and the prefrontal cortex. More specifically, the limbic system is the entire circuitry that controls your dog's emotional behaviour and motivational drive, and the parts controlling your dog's behaviour are the:

• **Amygdala:** Control of aggression, fear and tameness. It enables social cues to be picked up and is a key factor in memory and food intake. This part of the brain is the emotional control centre.

• **Cingulate gyrus:** Coordinates smell and sight. It is the interceptor of pain and aggression, and regulates tameness and motivation.

• **Hippocampus:** Long-term memory, spatial awareness and three-dimensional mapping.

• **Hypothalamus:** Important in fight/flight response, sexual behaviour, appetite, thirst, pleasure and rage.

• **Locus coereleus:** This is the control of anxiety-based responses and arousal.

• **Neocortex:** Important in memory.

• **Olfactory bulb:** Sensory processing (scent is known to trigger memories).

• **Raphe nuclei:** A combination of nuclei which house most of the serotonin-containing neurons. Controls mood and emotion, and coordinates sleep/wake cycles with the locus coereleus.

• **Thalamus:** A relay centre. Important in sexual orientation, and emotional and physical safety.

Neurotransmitters are chemical messengers, and various brain regions contain their receptors. Neurotransmitters important in behaviour include serotonin, GABA (calming), adrenalin, acetylcholine and dopamine (excitatory). These act to excite or calm the brain and thus influence behaviour. Some animals, for example, have insufficient calming neurotransmitters and exhibit anxiety-based behavioural abnormalities that require medication to rectify.

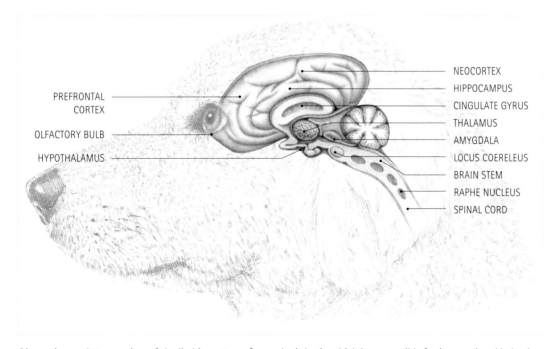

PREFRONTAL CORTEX

OLFACTORY BULB

HYPOTHALAMUS

NEOCORTEX

HIPPOCAMPUS

CINGULATE GYRUS

THALAMUS

AMYGDALA

LOCUS COERELEUS

BRAIN STEM

RAPHE NUCLEUS

SPINAL CORD

Above *A complete overview of the limbic system of your dog's brain which is responsible for its emotional behaviour and motivational drive.*

Above *Dogs can become sluggish on hot days, but lethargy can also be caused by illness.*
Right *Balancing the needs of your dog with your love of a well-maintained garden, can be a challenge at the best of times.*

PHYSIOLOGY

Changes in the health of an animal will often be reflected in its behaviour. Old dogs suffering from arthritis may exercise less and start to growl and snap when touched in certain areas, or if someone accidentally bumps and hurts it.

A dog that is unwell may hide away and sleep more than usual; one which is deaf may be easily startled if approached from behind or touched when asleep; while the dog that is unable to see well will tend to approach new people and objects tentatively. Some older dogs even suffer from mental deterioration, equivalent to that of Alzheimer's disease in humans, and become disorientated and vague (see pp102—103).

Hormonal changes are also reflected in behaviour. A bitch on heat will become more submissive and friendly, and will posture differently. One that has recently given birth may show uncharacteristic aggression when approached as she is defending her offspring.

Male dogs that have attained sexual maturity may become more pushy and aggressive, while some females that have been quite dominant and difficult as puppies may become more settled and less reactive after their first heat.

Dogs suffering from medical problems, such as thyroid dysfunction, may show behavioural changes. Those with decreased production of thyroid hormone (hypothyroidism) may be lethargic and are often aggressive. Once treated, these dogs show vastly improved behaviour.

ENVIRONMENT

The environment directly influences animal behaviour. On the most basic level, we can observe this when the weather changes. If it is very hot, most dogs will seek shade and will rest until it is cooler. They will then be more likely to play.

If it is wet and cold, many dogs are reluctant to brave the elements to go for their usual walk. Some are extremely frightened of thunderstorms and loud noises and will hide and tremble in response to them. Noise from building sites, such as staple guns and circular saws, can also cause distress, as can excessive traffic noise. This is a problem for some dogs, especially if there is nowhere for them to feel safe or take refuge.

A particular environment could also provoke certain behavioural traits. A dog that is suddenly taken to a farm and exposed to a field of sheep or wild rabbits could show predatory behaviour that might never have been triggered in its suburban environment.

Above *Border Collies are genetically programmed to herd. Most will do so even on their first encounter with animals such as the goat in this picture.*

Lack of stimulation within an environment can also have a profound effect on a dog's behaviour. Generally, those dogs that are left alone in a yard for extended periods of time with nothing to do, and that do not have regular long walks with off-lead exercise, tend to become hyper-reactive to stimuli. As a result they tend to bark at the slightest provocation, such as the sound of birds in the garden, cars in the street and voices.

Most dogs instinctively guard their immediate home environment or territory. A dog left in a car while its owner is in a shop will usually guard the car and is likely to show aggression towards strangers. In other situations, for example, when out on a walk, it may ignore or even happily welcome the approach of strangers.

Most dogs respond well to a predictable routine as this makes them feel secure. However, when major changes occur in their lifestyles, such as family members leaving, new partners arriving or people suddenly going back to work after being at home for a long period of time, some dogs are unable to cope and become very stressed and anxious (see Chapter 8).

Above *Most dogs are known to be fiercely protective of their owners' vehicles and may, without warning, show aggression towards strangers approaching them.*
Left *Dogs left alone for long periods of time with lack of exercise and stimulation may become stressed and anxious, and bark incessantly as a result.*

PAST EXPERIENCES

Dogs that are exposed to different situations while they are puppies cope better with suburban life than those that are kept isolated from a young age. Introducing puppies to car travel, public areas and other animals while they are most open to environmental exploration and learning makes life easier for them and their owners in the future, provided these early experiences are positive.

There are certain critical periods, coinciding with puppies' developmental phases, during which they should be exposed to human contact and to other puppies. If they do not receive this contact, they can develop behavioural problems later on in life.

Dogs that have been hurt or frightened in certain situations will react fearfully when exposed to similar situations in the future because they have formed a fear memory. This memory can be triggered by sight, sound or smell cues. Examples of this include pain experienced during a visit to the veterinary surgeon, and distress caused by having been exposed to a house fire or a car accident.

Above *Dogs that have been teased by passing children may become quite aggressive towards children in general.*

Similarly, the dog that has been repeatedly teased and poked at by school children passing in front of its gate at home is likely to become quite intolerant of young people. Not only has it learned to expect challenge from children, it has also learned that growling and snarling at them will cause them to leave (they are leaving anyway to continue on to school or home). In this way, the dog's aggressive behaviour is constantly reinforced.

Your Dog's Development

In order to be competent dog owners, it is important that we understand what to expect from our dogs, and to help us understand them it is useful to look at the world from a dog's perspective. Although dogs can live in harmony with people and have a similar social structure, their perception of the environment is very different as their acute senses of smell and hearing allow them to receive sensory information that we find impossible to detect. This may also cause owners to misinterpret their dog's behaviour as may be the case when they think their dog is barking for no reason when, in fact, it is responding to disturbing sounds it has detected. Understanding how vastly your dog's conception of its surroundings differs from yours is important in allowing you to relate to, train and manage your dog sympathetically and successfully.

Left *Remember that dogs need plenty of exercise away from their own property, and lots of interactive play with balls and other toys.*

THE SENSES

A dog's sense of smell is extremely sensitive, its hearing is acute and its vision is adapted to detect the slightest of movements. These physiological attributes mean that your dog receives sensory input from the environment of which humans are totally unaware.

TASTE

The most abundant form of taste buds in dogs are Group A taste receptors. Amino acids trigger the strongest responses in these taste buds which also respond to sugars such as fructose, sucrose and some artificial sweeteners.

Dogs also have Group B taste receptors which respond to water and to some amino acids, Group C receptors which respond to meaty flavours and Group D receptors which are triggered by fruity flavours. This all makes sense when we consider that dogs are not strict carnivores. They enjoy fruit, some vegetables, grains and dairy products.

Dogs vary tremendously in their individual taste preferences, although all of them will avoid acidic or sour foods. In general dogs prefer canned meat to fresh, cooked meat and raw meat, and prefer meat in general to cereal.

SCENT

Of all domestic animals, the dog has the most sensitive sense of smell. With up to 230 million olfactory cells, it can detect odours at a level of 1 in 10,000,000.

When you walk your dog, it is receiving messages by means of scents which you cannot even begin to detect. This is a very important means of communication for your dog. Glands that secrete odiferous substances are located around the head, neck and perineal area. This is why dogs sniff at those spots when they meet.

Below *Police dogs are well known for their acute sense of smell; they can detect human scent and narcotic substances over very long distances.*

THE SCENT ORGANS OF THE DOG

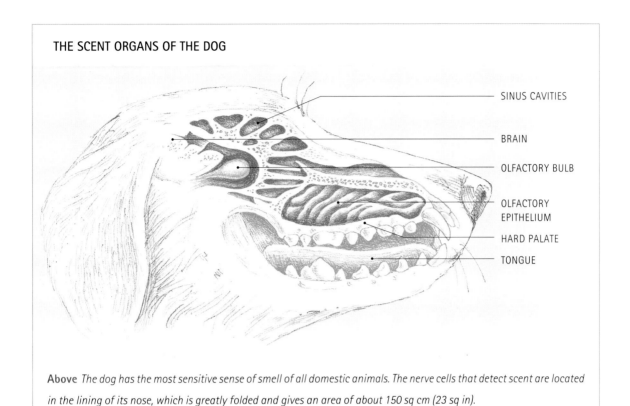

SINUS CAVITIES

BRAIN

OLFACTORY BULB

OLFACTORY EPITHELIUM

HARD PALATE

TONGUE

Above *The dog has the most sensitive sense of smell of all domestic animals. The nerve cells that detect scent are located in the lining of its nose, which is greatly folded and gives an area of about 150 sq cm (23 sq in).*

Two major glands situated on each side of the anus produce a strong-smelling secretion that coats the faeces, leaving a message for other dogs that persists for some time.

These secretions are different in each individual, thus when your dog sniffs at faeces on the roadside, it is learning about the social status of the dog that left it there and the time this occurred. Urine is also full of information for your dog. It provides clues about which other dog passed by, how long ago and its reproductive status. You may find it irritating that your dog insists on sniffing around lampposts, but remember, it is gaining important information by doing this.

A difficult aspect of training is to teach your dog to focus only on you and your requirements, and to ignore all this environmental stimulation.

Right *The Dachshund is gaining important information from gland secretions in its first encounter with this dog.*

HEARING

Interpretation using sound is important among dogs, especially in situations where their vision may be impaired, such as in thick undergrowth. Their hearing is acute with a range of 20,000 to 65,000hz, which means dogs can hear fainter sounds than humans can. A sound, which is only just audible to a human standing 6m (7yd) from its source, can be heard by most dogs at a distance of 25m (27yd).

They can also pick up the sound of an approaching thunderstorm 10km (6 miles) away and may become restless, pacing and whining well before the storm arrives.

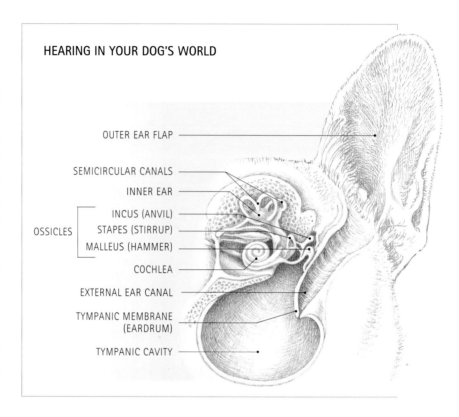

HEARING IN YOUR DOG'S WORLD

OUTER EAR FLAP

SEMICIRCULAR CANALS

INNER EAR

INCUS (ANVIL)

STAPES (STIRRUP)

OSSICLES

MALLEUS (HAMMER)

COCHLEA

EXTERNAL EAR CANAL

TYMPANIC MEMBRANE (EARDRUM)

TYMPANIC CAVITY

High-pitched sounds that are generally not a problem for people can also really bother dogs. Smoke alarms are a good example: their high-pitched beeps cause many dogs to tremble and hide.

Acute hearing in canines adds to their value as guard dogs as they can detect the presence of intruders on their property well before their owners notice anything. This acute hearing also enables them to obey commands over long distances, such as when they are working stock on the farm. It may also explain restless behaviour in dogs and why at times they seem to be barking at nothing obvious.

Left *Most dogs, such as this German Shepherd, have such a keen sense of hearing that they can detect faint sounds 25m (27yd) away.*

SIGHT

Although a dog's binocular vision is poor, its lateral vision is good, detecting subtle movements. It can see hand signals 1km (½ mile) away but has limited colour vision.

A dog's vision matures at about four months of age. Prior to this, objects may appear blurred, which could explain the unprovoked fearful behaviour that is sometimes observed in puppies.

Visual signals are an important part of canine communication. Their posture, ear and tail positions, movements and hair pattern communicate their mood and intention.

Your dog will react to subtle changes in body language, both human and canine, that you may not have even noticed. This would explain why your dog suddenly growls at an approaching stranger.

Right *Because puppies have blurred vision in the first four months, they can be anxious of and frightened by unidentified shapes looming in front of them.*

THE SIGHT ORGANS OF THE DOG

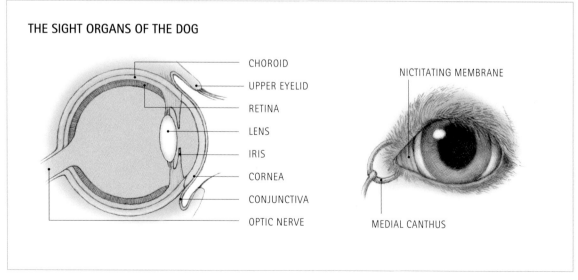

CHOROID

UPPER EYELID

RETINA

LENS

IRIS

CORNEA

CONJUNCTIVA

OPTIC NERVE

NICTITATING MEMBRANE

MEDIAL CANTHUS

THE CANINE SOCIAL SYSTEM

Dogs are regarded as communal animals. To interact successfully in this way, they rely on a hierarchy. This means that there is a pack leader and the other pack members are ranked progressively at levels below this leader. High-ranking animals are deferred to by those of lower rank and receive priority access to preferred resources such as food and favoured sleeping areas.

This hierarchy is maintained without constant fighting by a system of communication or social signalling. A lower-ranking animal will approach one of higher standing with its head down, gaze averted, tail down and wagging, and ears back. When approached by a higher-ranking animal, it may roll on its side exposing its throat and stomach.

Below *Dogs maintain social harmony with a system of social signalling. Here the submissive dog rolls over exposing vulnerable body areas, indicating that it is no threat at all to the dominant animal.*

While this body language indicates complete submission in the lower ranks, higher-ranking animals maintain an upright posture with straight tail and direct gaze.

Young animals growing up in the group need to find their place in the hierarchy. They do this by testing response to challenge. They may refuse to move out of the way of a higher-ranking dog or refuse to give up a bone to it. The higher-ranking animal will usually respond by growling and assuming a threatening posture. If the young animal doesn't back down, a fight may ensue and the youngster very quickly learns its boundaries. Once the relationship is clearly defined, there is usually no further trouble. In fact, in most cases, signalling from the adult or higher-ranking member generally is sufficient to cause the youngster to back down and respect its limits without a fight.

When a dog lives with humans, it needs to know where it stands in the hierarchy of the household. If there is confusion over this, problems can arise as the dog may challenge human family members to gain feedback on its relative social standing.

COMMUNICATION

Dogs communicate mood and intention with body postures such as head, ear and tail positions, and hair patterns, as well as vocally with howls, barks, whines and whimpers. They use scent as well, gaining information from glandular secretions and urine.

When your dog is reacting aggressively, note that it stands upright with its ears pricked forward, tail up and straight – possibly even wagging – with hair standing up on its neck and shoulders. Its teeth are also slightly bared. On the other hand, when your dog is approaching you in a friendly manner, its head is level or slightly lower than its shoulders. Its ears are relaxed, often back, tail in a relaxed position, wagging, and hair flat. When your dog is fearful, however, it most likely has its ears flat against its head, tail tucked between its legs and body low to the ground. It may crouch or roll over onto its side, and its hair may be raised on its neck and rump.

Your dog's barking is also a good form of communication over distance. It is used to convey messages to neighbouring animals and to alert members of the pack, human

Above When dogs are happy to interact with each other, they convey this willingness with their body postures and facial expressions. The dog on the right is less confident than the Golden Retriever.

or canine, to the presence of intruders and potential dangers. It is also used as a threat to warn off intruders.

Your dog's barking also varies in tone and intensity according to its purpose. You may have noticed that it reacts to a neighbouring dog's barking at some times and not others. It seems that the type of bark is important. If the neighbouring dog is greeting its owners, your dog will not react. If, however, it is barking at an intruder, your dog will become agitated and join in the territorial defence.

Furthermore, your dog's whimpers and whines are used for close communication with you and other dogs to express concern and to seek attention. Howls are used over long distances to communicate with other dogs, and sometimes with people. They are used more by some breeds than others.

YOUR DOG'S GROWTH PHASES

Puppies

At birth puppies are blind, deaf, and have very limited mobility. Even at this early age they compete for access to their mother's teats. In large litters, where not all the puppies can feed at one time, the strongest or most determined will do best.

At around 10 days the eyes open and the ear canals become unblocked. By three weeks puppies begin to play. From three to five weeks, they make positive responses to the approach of any new individual. This is an important time for them to have contact with people. They experience a fear phase at eight weeks (see p124) so this is not a good time for them to leave the litter. A second fear phase occurs at around 14 weeks. Puppies that have been well socialized prior to this will probably not show much change. In some, however, the change in response to new events or strange people is quite dramatic. Owners need to help them through this by being patient and understanding.

Substrate preference develops at about seven to nine weeks of age which is a good time for puppies to go to a new home (see p61).

Puppies under four months of age need to pass urine approximately every two hours and defecate approximately four times daily. It is important to be vigilant and to take your puppy outside as soon as it shows signs of restlessness and sniffing at the ground. Make a point of taking it outside as soon as it awakes after every meal and after 10 minutes of vigorous play. Stay with it until it has eliminated, then praise it. Do not expect the puppy to take itself outside at a young age.

Young puppies cannot last for eight hours overnight without passing urine so make sure your puppy is taken out at 23:00 and 05:00 until it is four months old.

Young puppies need to eat regularly. They should be fed four times daily until three months of age, then three times a day until six months of age, then twice daily.

Above *Puppies are born blind and deaf and are entirely dependent on their mother's care.*
Left *The ideal age for puppies to leave the litter is between seven and nine weeks.*

The problem is that as humans we may not respond in the same way as the puppy's siblings do, so it does not receive feedback that it understands. If it bites a little too hard, a child may scream, move suddenly and flail his arms about. This excites the puppy and encourages it to continue.

It is best to keep young puppies and children under five years of age apart. Allow interaction between them only under strict supervision and have the child sit in a chair. Wait until the puppy is due for a rest and allow the child to quietly pat it.

Above *It is important that young puppies have contact with people especially when they are between three and five weeks of age.*
Right *Children should be taught how to handle puppies properly and to respect their needs.*

In a natural situation, pups stay in a family group for at least six months and often longer. During this time there is constant change in the relative dominance of individual puppies. A pup that is dominant at eight weeks may be submissive at 12 weeks.

Puppies learn from play. If a puppy bites too hard, the victim will yelp and refuse to have anything to do with it. In this way they learn to control the intensity of their play. A mother will discipline her puppies if they behave roughly. She will firmly place her mouth over a puppy's face to stop unacceptable behaviour, or she may push it onto its side and place a paw on its neck or shoulder.

When a puppy is adopted into a human household it regards humans as a replacement for its canine family members. It invites play and jumps, yaps and growls in the same way as it would do when playing with the litter. It is especially interested in encouraging young children to play; toddlers lying or sitting on the floor are ideal targets and it may be very persistent.

Training should begin as soon as the puppy arrives in its new home. Puppies learn very quickly at a young age. An eight-week-old puppy can learn how to sit on command within seven days.

Make sure that older children learn how to handle the puppy correctly. They should not roll around on the floor or wrestle with it in any way. They can play with it using a tug toy but should not tolerate the dog grabbing clothes or arms. If the puppy insists on ignoring toys and jumping at everyone, it should be told 'no' and left alone until it settles down. When it has settled, return to it, ask it to sit and reward good behaviour with a pat and a treat.

Offer the puppy its own toys and encourage play with these. Young puppies have a strong need to chew. This need is probably at its strongest at about four to six months of age, which coincides with the growth of adult teeth. Puppies have no way of knowing that they must not chew the furniture, your shoes, the towels or the carpet. They cannot distinguish between the child's teddy and their own soft toys. So it is up to you to keep valuable items out of harm's way. Ensure that the puppy has its own toys to chew. If it does start to chew something that it shouldn't, take the object away and replace it with one of the puppy's chew toys. When you cannot supervise the puppy, make sure that it is confined to a safe area with its own toys around it.

Digging is a natural behaviour for pups and adult dogs (see p60). Discourage your puppy from digging in your favourite flowerbed by providing it with a sandpit and encouraging it to dig only in that area.

Crate training

Crate training, providing your puppy with a small, secure area containing a bed and toys, can be helpful in house training. This can take the form of a playpen, a large travelling cage or a blocked off corner of a room. The puppy can sleep in the area overnight, and can be placed in there during the day when direct supervision is not possible.

Below *A tug toy is a source of interactive play, and prevents puppies tugging on your clothes or soft furnishings.*

Puppies are less likely to soil in their bed area and will usually vocalize when they need to eliminate. They still need to be taken out regularly (every two hours as young pups) during the day, before and after feeding, and after five to 10 minutes of play. They are less likely to make mistakes inside your home using this system because they cannot wander off to some corner unnoticed.

This system should be used until your puppy is fully house-trained (usually by four months). The enclosure should then be left open for it to come and go at leisure. Most puppies choose to return to it to sleep.

Crate training has the advantage of providing puppies with an area where they feel safe and it accustoms them to spending time alone instead of constantly following their owners around the house. This can help to prevent separation anxiety (see Chapter 8).

Adolescents

Puppies reach sexual maturity at six to eight months. They are not socially mature, however, until they are 18 months old. Much like teenagers, they are likely to challenge family members over favoured objects or areas to gain feedback on where they stand in the social hierarchy of the household.

People often have difficulty coping with their dogs between the ages of six to twelve months. Dogs tend to be extremely active at this time and are keen to explore every aspect of their environment. This is the time when owners start to complain about their washing being dragged off the line, shoes being stolen from the back door, and enormous holes being dug in the backyard.

It does get better! The important thing is to ensure the dog gets plenty of exercise off the property and lots of interactive play with balls and other toys during the day. There should be a daily training session where all the commands are practised. Undesirable behaviour should be redirected to desirable behaviour. Be consistent with training.

It is important for young dogs to have clear guidelines and feedback about their position in the household,

Above *Puppies delight in interactive play. Washing flapping on the line is irresistible, as they can chase it as it blows about, swing on it and even tear it up!*

especially as they reach the age of 18 months. If this does not happen, they are likely to challenge family members to gain their feedback. This can result in injury and a serious breakdown in the dog-human relationship.

Preferably, all family members should establish a higher social rank than the dog or dogs. This is achieved by behaving in ways that demand deference from the dog. Family members should occasionally sit on the dog's bed or in its favourite area. This will prevent it from becoming overprotective of these highly desirable spots.

From puppyhood, the dog should be fed at least one of its meals after the family has eaten. This equates to the pack situation where dominant members eat first and subordinates move in later. The dog should also be asked to sit and wait while people pass through doorways first. Most importantly, people should maintain an upright posture around the dog.

Lying on the floor and allowing the dog to stand over you, as children often do in play, is interpreted as subordinate behaviour and could lead to aggression from the dog when you later try to discipline it.

It is common for a young dog to indulge in frequent attention-seeking behaviour such as pawing at family members, pushing under arms, clambering onto knees and barking, and this can occur at any time the dog wishes to control a situation such as when its owners are preoccupied with television or are having a conversation.

This behaviour should be totally ignored and the dog should be given attention only after it has moved away and is sitting quietly. Once the dog has obeyed its command to sit, the owner should only then fuss over, or reward it for good behaviour. The attention should stop when the owner has had enough. If the dog asks for a game, that's fine, but the owner decides when the game stops. Some dogs will continue ad nauseam pushing toys at owners who need to learn to ignore this behaviour.

Adults

The adult dog that has been properly handled and trained as a puppy should have learned to fit in with its family's daily routine. It will look forward to its daily walks, will know exactly what time to expect its owner (or family members) to return home and will not allow you to forget its dinner time. It will probably enjoy riding in the car and will recognize streets and destinations. It will be happiest when the whole family is together.

An adult dog usually defecates twice daily. Urine may be passed on home ground when necessary but tends to be used for marking during walks as dogs love to gather information about the environment. They need to be allowed to sniff and contemplate. They also like to interact with other dogs. If your dog walks on regular routes or goes to the park every day, it will make particular friends with whom it likes to play.

Left *Dogs love to ride in the car and to be involved in family outings. However, to help them familiarize themselves with the car and to counter motion sickness, you need to start taking them for short rides from an early age. Dogs that continue to get sick despite frequent trips in the car, may need to be medicated and should be seen by a veterinary surgeon.*

When two dogs meet for the first time, they will approach each other cautiously with heads outstretched and wagging tails. They will move to each other's side and sniff around the respective cheek area. Then they will progress to sniffing at the groin region and around the tail. Owners should allow their dogs to do this. The two dogs will then either move on, invite play or growl and posture aggressively. If the latter should occur, it is safest for the owners to separate their dogs swiftly and calmly.

Occasionally a dog out walking may take exception to an approaching pedestrian. This may be related to the person's body posture or scent. Learn to read your dog's signals (stiffening of the body, ears forward and hair standing up on the neck and possibly the rump) and ask it to sit quietly

Above *Most family outings and annual vacations can be extended to include dogs as they can easily learn to behave well, in a safe manner, in cars and even in boats.*

while the person passes. Place yourself between the dog and the approaching person.

Most dogs like to be occupied during the day and, if left alone for long periods, will become frustrated and bored, amusing themselves by digging holes, chewing shoes inadvertently left outside, or barking at passers-by. If you have to leave your dog alone for long periods, make sure it has a good walk first (preferably of a one-hour duration), a comfortable bed, access to shelter and interesting toys.

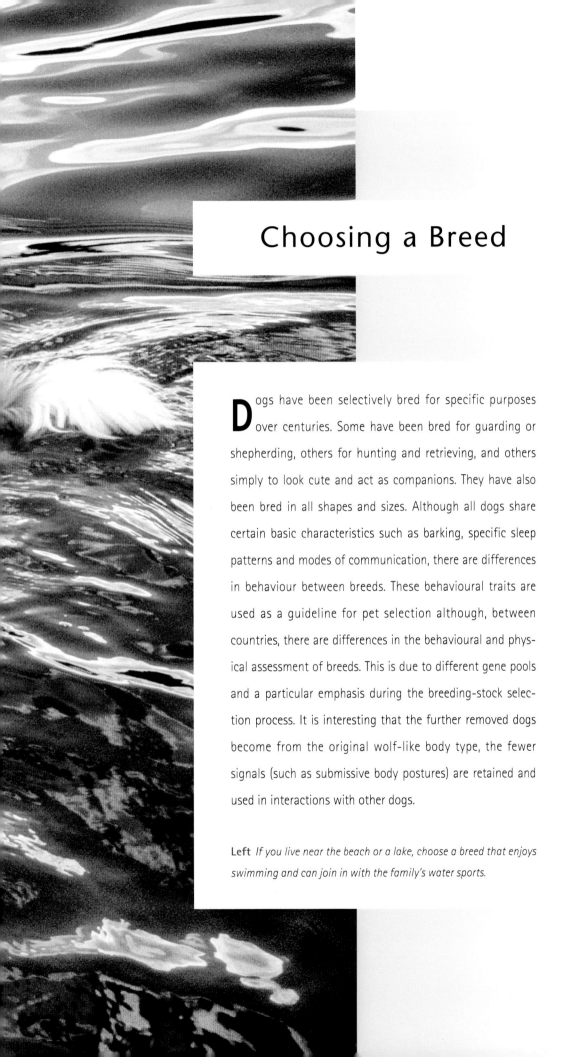

Choosing a Breed

Dogs have been selectively bred for specific purposes over centuries. Some have been bred for guarding or shepherding, others for hunting and retrieving, and others simply to look cute and act as companions. They have also been bred in all shapes and sizes. Although all dogs share certain basic characteristics such as barking, specific sleep patterns and modes of communication, there are differences in behaviour between breeds. These behavioural traits are used as a guideline for pet selection although, between countries, there are differences in the behavioural and physical assessment of breeds. This is due to different gene pools and a particular emphasis during the breeding-stock selection process. It is interesting that the further removed dogs become from the original wolf-like body type, the fewer signals (such as submissive body postures) are retained and used in interactions with other dogs.

Left *If you live near the beach or a lake, choose a breed that enjoys swimming and can join in with the family's water sports.*

I frequently see sad situations where dogs are being re-homed because people did not give enough thought to the type of dog suitable for their circumstances. In some cases these people should not have considered getting a dog at all. The case of Teddy provides a good example of owner-breed mismatch. Teddy was a Lakeland Terrier.

At nine months of age, Terry was driving his owners mad. He was presented to the behaviour clinic with a history of nipping at the teenage boys in the household, growling when anyone walked near his food bowl while he was eating, and running away when off his lead. On several occasions he had nipped at children playing in the street.

Teddy's owners also complained that he was aloof and didn't greet them with licks and a wagging tail when they returned home. On occasion, he might fetch a toy and invite play, but he was not one to lavish affection upon the family. Having had a spaniel prior to Teddy, the owners missed the greeting behaviour and felt rejected by the little dog.

Being a terrier, Teddy liked to dig and bark. He was very lively and excitable. Whenever anyone was working outside in the garden, Teddy would join in, barking ferociously at the spades and brooms, and doing his own excavating.

When the family had builders working on the property, Teddy would drop a bone in front of them and growl at them if they went anywhere near it.

Teddy was a dominant dog, determined to work his way up in the hierarchy of the household. He needed stability, a firm hand, clear signals and daily training sessions. The family were all very busy. The boys had lots of friends and there was a constant stream of teenagers in and out of the house at weekends. This was difficult for Teddy to deal with and he became very excited and almost distressed when lots of strangers were present.

No one really had the time or the inclination to work with Teddy in a way that would get results. The parents wanted to spend summer weekends at their holiday home but felt that taking Teddy would prevent them from relaxing fully. He was likely to wander off because the holiday property was not fenced. If they tied him up, he would bark and that would disturb them and the neighbours. The teenage boys could not be depended upon to care for him properly if he was left at home.

Teddy's owners had not thought clearly enough about the role a dog would play in their plans. They had forgotten how much work is involved in training a young dog and had assumed the teenage family members would take more responsibility for the dog than, in fact, they did.

They chose the breed because it was cute, curly and unusual. They were not aware of how different terriers and spaniels could be. They did not know that as a breed, Lakeland Terriers are aloof and independent. They also did not notice how dominant the parent animals were. Fortunately, Teddy was re-homed to a family living on a farm. The family had always had terriers and loved them dearly. They were happy to take Teddy, warts and all!

Left *Dogs with a high reactivity level and a strong predatory drive such as these Blood-hounds may not make good family pets.*

The case of Teddy reinforces the fact that due consideration should be given to the breed of dog when selecting one to suit your lifestyle. When doing so, it may be useful to consider parameters such as reactivity (response rate and intensity to stimuli), aggressiveness (hostile or destructive behaviour), immaturity (puppy-like behaviour such as submissiveness and playfulness) and predatory drive (an innate response to prey species):

• Reactivity — Highly reactive dogs tend to be very territorial and may bark frequently. They may also be demanding of attention and will probably need lots of exercise and stimulation.

• Aggressiveness — Aggressive breeds may be good guard dogs but may tend to be dominant and may not be appropriate for a family situation.

• Immaturity — Breeds showing high immaturity scores may be very dependent on their owners and, as a result, should not be left alone for long periods of time. They are also likely to be good in family situations.

• Predatory drive — Dogs with high predatory drives are likely to chase, and may kill small animals and/or livestock. In some cases, as previously discussed, this behaviour can even be directed towards children.

It is important to remember that not every individual

Above *Dogs with low reactivity and high immaturity levels may be best suited to elderly people. Owning a dog often provides the aged with a new interest, but it is important that the pet be manageable.*

animal is going to be typical of its breed. Having chosen a breed that may suit you, it is important that, when selecting an individual of that breed, the parent animals appeal to you, and then by visiting the litter several times and observing the individual puppies.

Good family dogs	High-energy dogs	Low-energy dogs	Guard dogs
Boxer	Beagle	Bichon Frise	Dalmatian
Bichon Frise	Border Collie	Cavalier King Charles	Doberman
Cavalier King Charles	Boxer	Spaniel	German Shepherd
Spaniel	Cocker Spaniel	Dachshund	Rottweiler
Dalmatian	Dalmatian	Labrador Retriever	Schnauzer
Golden Retriever	Doberman	Poodle	Rhodesian Ridgeback
Labrador Retriever	German Shepherd	Pug	
Poodle	Jack Russell Terrier	West Highland White	
Pug	Labrador Retriever	Terrier	
Rhodesian Ridgeback	Springer Spaniels	Rhodesian Ridgeback	
	Staffordshire Bull Terrier		

Australian Cattle Dog

Active, intelligent, quick to learn.
Tendency to nip and may show strong
predatory drive. Territorial. May retrieve.

Country of origin: Australia
Date of origin: 1800s
Life expectancy: 12 years
Weight range: 16–20kg (35–44 lb)
Height range: 43–51cm (17–20in)
First use: Cattle herding
Use today: Cattle herding, companion

Beagle

Bright, active, high activity level, moderate
to high predatory drive, tends to be dominant.
Moderate trainability. Generally not suitable
as a suburban dog due to its need for large
amounts of exercise and tendency to wander
off, following scent. Needs company and is
prone to separation anxiety.

Country of origin: Great Britain
Date of origin: 1300s
Life expectancy: 13 years
Weight range: 8–14kg (18–31 lb)
Height range: 33–41cm (13–16in)
First use: Rabbit/hare hunting
Use today: Companion, gun dog, field trials

Bichon Frise

Good-natured, low to moderate activity level, low reactivity, good with children and other animals but tends to trigger aggression in other breeds. Low predatory drive. Lively and affectionate. Very dependent. Can be highly vocal.

Country of origin: Mediterranean region
Date of origin: Middle Ages
Life expectancy: 14 years
Weight range: 3–6kg (7–13 lb)
Height range: 23–30cm (9–12in)
First use: Companion
Use today: Companion

Border Collie

Highly intelligent, quick to train, high activity level, high reactivity, high predatory drive but does not kill. Will round up any livestock including birds. Tendency to snap at noses! Not particularly good with children. Best for smallholdings, farms or very active owners. Often reserved or timid with strangers.

Country of origin: Great Britain
Date of origin: 1700s
Life expectancy: 12–14 years
Weight range: 14–22kg (31–49 lb)
Height range: 46–54cm (18–21in)
First use: Shepherd/cattle herding
Use today: Companion, sheep herding, sheepdog trials

Boxer

High activity level, high reactivity, low aggression, easy to train if not in company but can be easily distracted and excitable in group situations. Low predatory drive. Good family dogs if the children are over 10 years of age and the family is physically active. Good guard dogs, vocal about intruders but won't rush·in to bite them.

Country of origin: Germany
Date of origin: 1850s
Life expectancy: 12 years
Weight range: 25–32kg (55–71 lb)
Height range: 53–63cm (21–25in)
First use: Guarding, bull baiting
Use today: Companion

Cavalier King Charles Spaniel

Low to moderate activity level. Low reactivity, low aggression. Needs company. Breed predisposition to obsessive-compulsive disorders. Good with children. Low predatory drive. Moderate trainability. High immaturity. Good companion for elderly people, as it is happy to sit beside its owners or on their knees for considerable amounts of time.

Country of origin: Great Britain
Date of origin: 1925
Life expectancy: 9–14 years
Weight range: 5–8kg (11–18 lb)
Height range: 31–33cm (12–13in)
First use: Companion
Use today: Companion

Dachshund

Moderate activity level. Moderate aggression, may be dominant. Moderate reactivity. Doesn't retrieve. Low to moderate trainability. Not always good with children. Tends to bark and dig. Long-haired animals seem to be more reserved than those with short or wire coats.

Country of origin: Germany

Date of origin: 1900s

Life expectancy: 14–17 years

Weight range:

(miniature) 4–5kg (9–11 lb)

(standard) 7–12kg (15–26 lb)

Height range: (miniature and standard) 13–25cm (5–10in)

First use: Badger flushing

Use today: Companion

Dalmatian

High activity, high reactivity, moderate to high aggression, low predatory drive. These dogs have huge exercise requirement and really need to run. Good family dog and guard dog. High trainability. Good for agility. Likes to retrieve. Good with horses and other animals.

Country of origin: Balkans

Date of origin: Middle Ages

Life expectancy: 12–14 years

Weight range: 23–25kg (51–55 lb)

Height range: 50–61cm (20–24in)

First use: Hunting, carriage dog

Use today: Companion

Doberman

High activity level, high reactivity, moderate to high aggression, may be dominant. Good guard dog, loyal to owner and family, may not be good with strangers. High trainability. Not good with young children.

Country of origin: Germany
Date of origin: 1800s
Life expectancy: 12 years
Weight range: 30–40kg (66–88 lb)
Height range: 65–69cm (26–27in)
First use: Guarding
Use today: Companion, security

English Springer Spaniel

Moderate to high activity level, high reactivity, moderate trainability and moderate predatory drive. Bred as a gun dog.
Retrieves well. Likes water.

Country of origin: Great Britain
Date of origin: 1600s
Life expectancy: 12–14 years
Weight range: 22–24kg (49–53 lb)
Height range: 48–51cm (19–20in)
First use: Game flushing, retrieving
Use today: Companion, gun dog

German Shepherd

Moderate activity level. Moderate reactivity. Moderate to high aggression. Excellent guard dog. May be dominant. Tends to attach intensely to one person but can be a good family dog. Can retrieve. Moderate to strong predatory drive. Highly trainable. Cautious with approaching strangers.

Country of origin: Germany
Date of origin: 1800s
Life expectancy: 12–13 years
Weight range: 34–43kg (75–95 lb)
Height range: 55–66cm (22–26in)
First use: Sheep herding
Use today: Companion, security, police dog

Golden Retriever

Moderate activity level. Low reactivity. Low aggression, very gentle. Moderate to high trainability. Good retrieval skills. Good with children, excellent family pet. Low predatory drive. Likes water. Friendly towards strangers and happy to wander off with someone new.

Country of origin: Great Britain
Date of origin: 1800s
Life expectancy: 13–15 years
Weight range: 27–36kg (60–79 lb)
Height range: 51–61cm (20–24in)
First use: Game retrieving
Use today: Companion, gun dog, field trials, guide dog

Jack Russell Terrier

High activity level. High reactivity level. Strong predatory drive. May retrieve. Moderate to high aggression. Moderate trainability. May be dominant. Not ideal for suburban living unless with very active owners. Not especially child tolerant. Often enjoys boats and water, has been known to dive for fish!

Country of origin: Great Britain
Date of origin: 1800s
Life expectancy: 13–14 years
Weight range: 5–8kg (11–18 lb)
Height range: 28–38cm (11–15in)
First use: Ratting
Use today: Companion, ratting

Labrador Retriever

Moderate activity level. Moderate to low reactivity. Low to moderate aggression, may be a good guard. Good family pet. Highly trainable. Retrieves well. Very food oriented. Low to moderate predatory drive. Usually likes water. Good with strangers.

Country of origin: Great Britain
Date of origin: 1800s
Life expectancy: 12–14 years
Weight range: 25–34kg (55–75 lb)
Height range: 54–57cm (22–23in)
First use: Gun dog
Use today: Companion, gun dog, field trials, guide dog

Schnauzer

Moderate to high activity. Moderate to high reactivity. Moderate trainability. A good guard dog. Likes to bark. Tends to be dominant. Is not good with young children but a great companion for those over 10 years of age. Can retrieve but not noted for this.

Country of origin: Germany
Date of origin: Middle Ages
Life expectancy: 12–14 years
Weight range: 15–16kg (33–35 lb)
Height range: 45–50cm (18–20in)
First use: Ratting, guard dog
Use today: Companion

Scottish Terrier

Low to moderate activity. Moderate reactivity. Low trainability. Not good with children. Low to moderate predatory drive.

Country of origin: Great Britain
Date of origin: 1800s
Life expectancy: 13–14 years
Weight range: 9–11kg (20–24 lb)
Height range: 25–28cm (10–11in)
First use: Small-mammal hunting
Use today: Companion

Staffordshire Bull Terrier

High activity. High reactivity. High aggression towards other dogs but usually very friendly and reliable with people. Moderate trainability. May retrieve but not noted for this. Good with children. Moderate predatory drive.

Country of origin: Great Britain

Date of origin: 1800s

Life expectancy: 11–12 years

Weight range: 11–17kg (24–38 lb)

Height range: 36–41cm (14–16in)

First use: Dog fighting, ratting

Use today: Companion

Shetland Sheepdog

Moderate to high activity. High reactivity. High trainability. A good guard. Good with children. Gentle, sensitive. Low predatory drive. High immaturity.

Country of origin: Great Britain

Date of origin: 1700s

Life expectancy: 12–14 years

Weight range: 6–7kg (14–16 lb)

Height range: 35–37cm (14–15in)

First use: Sheep herding

Use today: Companion, sheep herding

Siberian Husky

High activity. High reactivity. Playful. Not a good guard. Tendency to dominate. Often howl. High predatory drive.

Country of origin: Siberia

Date of origin: Antiquity

Life expectancy: 11–13 years

Weight range: 16–27kg (35–60 lb)

Height range: 51–60cm (20–24in)

First use: Sled pulling

Use today: Companion, sled racing

West Highland White Terrier

Moderate activity. Moderate reactivity. Low to moderate aggression. Will guard. Moderate trainability, can be strong-willed. Moderate predatory drive. Used in dog agility competitions in which dogs perform tasks such as running over narrow beams, jumping fences and water. In America they are used in earth dog trials in which either prey or objects are dug from holes in the ground. They make good family dogs.

Country of origin: Great Britain

Date of origin: 1800s

Life expectancy: 14 years

Weight range: 7–10kg (15–22 lb)

Height range: 25–28cm (10–11in)

First use: Ratting

Use today: Companion

Common Problems

Behavioural problems in dogs may be divided into two main categories: actions such as barking or digging that are normal but problematic because they disturb owners or neighbours, and actions such as shadow chasing and tail biting that are not normal but rather arise from abnormalities in the brain. The division between normal and abnormal behaviour is not always clear. A dog, for example, may be barking at neighbours or birds during the day because it feels like it and is blissfully unaware that its owners or neighbours find the behaviour irritating; or it may be barking because it is suffering from separation anxiety. Evaluation by an expert is required to differentiate between normal and abnormal behaviour. Common problems that arise from normal behaviour include barking, digging, destructive behaviour, guarding, house soiling, mounting and wandering.

Left *Some dogs are great escape artists and will go to any lengths to free themselves if shut in.*

BARKING

Barking is normal behaviour for dogs. It is a means of self-expression and communication. Dogs will bark to ward off intruders, to communicate with other dogs, to express excitement and pleasure during a ball game, when their owners arrive home, or prior to a walk. This is all perfectly normal and neighbours should accept this in moderation just as they accept that children will scream and shout when playing in the street after school.

Barking becomes a problem when it is excessive. It is probably the behaviour least tolerated by people, especially in urban areas. Excessive barking in a normal dog usually results from boredom or territorial (guarding) behaviour. Dogs that are left at home for long periods of time with nothing to do and are not walked daily will become extremely bored. Even if their backyard is huge, they know every inch of it and it simply isn't exciting anymore.

When dogs are bored they become hyper-reactive, and will then bark at the slightest stimulus. Birds in the trees are a favourite, and any faint noise may easily provoke them.

These dogs need to have more exercise. They should be taken out twice daily for 30 to 60 minutes. They should also have interactive play sessions as well as some good obedience training. A sandpit in which they may dig provides good interactive play. Remember also to rotate toys on a daily basis to stimulate their interest.

Providing a canine companion for a bored or lonely dog may decrease its motivation to bark as the animals can play together and keep each other company.

Some dogs are excessively territorial and will probably bark frequently during the day in defence of their territory particularly if their owner's property looks out onto a busy pavement. These dogs are to be differentiated, however, from those that bark incessantly in a monotone during the day from the moment their owners leave the house as they may be suffering from separation anxiety (see Chapter 8). These dogs need professional help. In fact, all problem-barking needs to be properly evaluated, and behaviour modification, in addition to novel stimuli, needs to be implemented. Note that anti-bark collars (see pp68–69) should not be used as a quick-fix treatment.

Below *Your dog's excessive barking may indicate a deeper problem and should be analyzed by an animal behaviourist.*

The case of Ronnie the barking Border Collie is a good example of how nuisance-barking may be treated.

Ronnie was a seven-year-old Border Collie whose owner contacted the behaviour clinic because the neighbours complained about the dog barking during the day.

Ronnie's owner, who had recently retired from farming, was at a loss to explain the situation because he seemed fine when the family left him in the morning and perfectly relaxed when they returned at night. He had frequently been alone on the farm and never seemed to bark much on those occasions.

A video-and-sound system set up to monitor Ronnie during the course of the day showed that he would rush out and bark when he saw neighbours in the garden or when people passed by the front fence. He also barked at and chased birds that landed anywhere on the property. Ronnie was taken for a 30-minute run at night and an hour's walk on Saturdays and Sundays.

Ronnie's problem was that he was a bright, active dog who suddenly found himself with nothing to do all day. He was not used to starting the day on a small section of land with nothing to do. To amuse himself he began to make up games. Barking at birds was satisfying because they always flew away. He soon learned that if he barked at the neighbours they would react. One neighbour used to throw biscuits over the fence, the other used to shout and throw sticks at him. The biscuits were always welcome and the sticks were amusing to chase and chew.

Ronnie was a normal but bored dog. He needed some changes to his routine. His owner was instructed to take him for a 30-minute run in the morning and one hour at night. He was provided with different toys including a food cube, a ball, chew bones and cardboard to tear up. Biscuits were hidden in the garden and Ronnie spent time tracking and extricating them.

A sandpit provided a place to dig, and toys and treats were buried in it. Ronnie was also taught fly ball and used to play this by himself during the day. A gate was erected so that he had no access to the front lawn and could not see pedestrians. The neighbours were instructed to ignore him and to stand still if he barked, moving on only when he was quiet.

Above *Boredom is common in many dogs who have nothing to occupy them, no stimulating living environment or no means to expend their energy.*

After one month on the new routine, Ronnie was no longer bothered about the birds or the neighbours. He was more relaxed, sleeping contentedly for the most part of the day.

If your dog has a barking problem, speak to a behaviourist. It is usually possible to rectify the situation with a modification programme. It is important that the cause of the barking is properly evaluated and treated.

DIGGING

Many dogs love to dig in the garden. They do so to bury bones and because it provides them with an interactive activity that is very stimulating, soil moves and responds when it is manipulated.

Some breeds such as terriers are more likely to dig than others because they have been selectively bred for this behaviour over several years. This is perfectly fine for the dog but may not be so well received by the owner particularly if the digging area is a prized vegetable garden or a carefully landscaped lawn.

Above *Digging is normal behaviour for dogs but can be very frustrating for owners if their plants are damaged.*
Left *Dogs can be taught to dig in their own sandpit rather than in the garden.*

Dogs can be taught to dig in certain areas; providing them with their own digging pit is also a good idea. If your dog insists on digging in unacceptable areas you can fence them off. If this is not practical, place an electric fence crisscrossed over the area you wish to keep dog-free. The dog will soon learn to avoid the area; the fence can then be removed and a single dummy string placed across the area to remind the dog to stay away.

Other ideas include filling holes with dog faeces or balloons. These methods work in many cases; however, some dogs think exploding a balloon is a great prize at the end of a dig! Snappy trainers, which are like plastic mousetraps that make a snapping noise when disturbed, can also act as a deterrent for some dogs.

DESTRUCTIVE BEHAVIOUR

All dogs go through a destructive phase as they grow (see p37). It is normal for puppies and young dogs to chew anything they can find and to tear up paper and cloth. Washing on the line is often a favourite target. This behaviour is usually under control by the time dogs reach 18 to 24 months of age.

Some dogs, however, seem to remain destructive. They need to be given a variety of their own toys to chew on and should receive large meaty bones to tear into. Cardboard boxes can be provided for them to destroy, too. These dogs should not have unsupervised access to the house. If they start to demolish a rug or chew at a tablecloth, they should be told 'no' and given their own chew-toy. If they insist on chewing the forbidden item, a water pistol can be used as a deterrent. In some instances it is useful to apply a commercial bandage protector spray (used to prevent dogs from biting at and removing bandages) to the object that the dog is favouring.

If a dog is destructive only when home alone and if the destruction is concentrated around doorways, the dog may be suffering from separation anxiety (see Chapter 8), so expert help should be obtained to evaluate the situation.

SOILING

Adult dogs that have been properly house-trained as puppies rarely soil inside the house. If your adult dog begins house soiling when it usually gives clear signals that it wants to be let out, or it has easy outdoor access, take it to the veterinary surgeon. It may have a bladder or bowel infection or may have developed incontinence.

Some dogs have an aversion to rain and frost and are reluctant to venture out to defecate during extremes of weather. Go outside with them with an umbrella or organize some covered area that they can use.

Male dogs that lift their leg inside could be marking territory and trying to assert dominance over members of the family or other dogs. This happens most commonly with newly adopted adult males. Neutering can achieve a 75 per cent reduction in this behaviour. Retraining is also necessary. The dog should be supervised constantly and startled with a foghorn or water pistol if he shows signs of lifting his leg. Dogs that have been adopted from kennels are often difficult to house-train because they have become used to soiling in their run area, in close proximity to their bed and on a hard surface that is similar to wooden flooring or linoleum. These dogs need retraining and the only way to do this is to follow puppy-training protocol. Take them outside regularly and remember to praise them when they defecate in the right place.

If areas of the house have become contaminated, clean them with an enzymatic cleaner (see p124). This eliminates

Right *To alleviate distress and boredom, dogs suffering from separation anxiety can become destructive and damage furniture and gardens, causing their owners unnecessary expense and frustration.*

traces of the odour stimulating the dog to soil again in the same spot despite the substrate being incorrect.

House soiling can also occur if a dog is frightened or suffers from separation anxiety (see p80). This increases their bowel activity and decreases their control over urination. Such dogs usually have other symptoms which makes it very important to correctly identify the cause of the problem.

Substrate preference

When puppies are able to urinate and defecate without the aid of their mother's stimulation, namely licking, they instinctively start to eliminate outside of their immediate nest area. At seven to nine weeks of age they develop a preference for certain surfaces on which to eliminate. These surfaces smell and feel right and when the puppy comes in contact with them, it is stimulated to urinate or defecate.

Most breeders use newspaper placed outside the nest and puppies become comfortable using this. The newspaper is then placed on grass in smaller and smaller pieces and finally removed. The puppy is thus stimulated to eliminate on grassed areas. It has developed a substrate preference, favouring grass for elimination.

Some breeders have already encouraged the puppies to start eliminating on grass before they go to their new homes, however, if they have not, using newspaper in the new home before introducing them to a more suitable substrate is not an essential step. Newly acquired puppies between the ages of seven and nine weeks quickly develop a substrate preference for whatever area they are consistently taken to and encouraged to use for this purpose.

MOUNTING

Puppies, both male and female, indulge in mounting behaviour during play; this is normal and has more to do with dominance than sex. This behaviour occurs commonly during puppy preschool meetings and should be ignored or the puppies distracted.

Dominant adolescent and adult females also sometimes exhibit mounting behaviour as do certain adolescent males, which make an attempt to mate every dog they meet and even show mounting and thrusting behaviour on cushions, sometimes even on their owners' or guests' legs. However, dogs that are well bonded to their owners tend not to do this. Training reduces this behaviour and castration of males decreases this behaviour by about 60 per cent.

If a dog is mounting, say 'no', walk away or remove the object in question. Redirect the dog to an acceptable activity. A water pistol can also be effective. Where the mounting behaviour is dominance-related, strategies must be put in place to reinforce the dog's subordination to you (see p95). If the behaviour does not stop, consider consulting an animal behaviourist.

WANDERING

Many owners complain that their dogs wander. The answer is to fence them in! Any dog is likely to follow its nose off the property. Wild dogs live in a group with a defended area (territory) in which their den is situated, and a home range over which they roam during hunting.

Below *Take the necessary measures to prevent your dog wandering, as it could get accidentally knocked over and hurt in a busy street.*

It is therefore natural for dogs to wander off their immediate property; it is impossible to teach the dog the idea of arbitrary boundaries, so they have to be tangible.

Some owners complain that their dog escapes the moment they open a gate or a front door to a visitor. The solution with these dogs is to pre-empt the behaviour; put them on a lead before you open the door or gate, or shut them in another room.

Make sure they have frequent off-property exercise, and lots of interactive play and training at home to make their place of residence fun and entertaining. Involve them in your daily chores; keep them occupied and practise calling them back to you, a technique known as recall, on a daily basis at home and when out walking. Remember to reward their return generously with food treats and physical praise.

Dogs that are well bonded tend not to stray too far from their owners. However, if the owners are out and the dog has no physical boundaries, it is likely to wander off out of boredom or to look for its missing pack members.

Castration of male dogs can decrease wandering by 90 per cent if it is done at a young age. A castrated male will have little interest in territorial marking and in locating a bitch on heat but if an adult dog is wandering because it can, castration will make no difference at all.

TERRITORIAL AGGRESSION: GUARDING

It is natural for dogs to guard territory. Most will bark to alert the family to the presence of a stranger and some will take it upon themselves to see the intruder off. This can be embarrassing, especially if the dog is happy to back up his bark with a bite!

Most dogs that have been well socialized can be taught to alert their owners to strangers and then back off. If your dog is overzealous in this behaviour, you need to teach it an alternative response to strangers. Here's how:

• Practise with a friend.

• Have your dog leashed and then ask your friend to ring the doorbell.

Above *The ability of dogs to guard their territory is an asset for dog owners, however, the dog must be controlled enough to stop and return to its owner when asked to do so.*

• Allow the dog to bark two or three times, then ask it to sit and look at you for a treat. Practise this until the dog starts to look to you for a treat when the doorbell rings.

• Ask your friend to enter the house, to ignore the dog, and then to take a seat.

• While your friend enters, the dog should be asked to sit quietly beside you about 4m (4.3yd) from the door.

• Once the person is seated, allow the dog to greet. Have treats available and ask your friend to tell the dog to sit in return for a treat.

• Ask the dog to sit quietly beside you while you talk to your friend.

This process takes time, and you will need to repeat this technique over a few weeks.

While you are training your dog, avoid unannounced guests. If someone does arrive unexpectedly during the early stages of training, do not panic. Instead, shut the dog in another room before it has a chance to show aggressive behaviour towards your guest.

Managing your Dog

To own a well-adjusted, well-behaved dog with which you can enjoy and share life requires a considerable investment of time and energy on your part. It is important to prepare yourself as much as possible prior to purchasing it. Keeping up to date on the latest information on dog training and behaviour will enable you to gain an understanding of what to expect from your dog as it grows and develops, much as you do when rearing a child. If you are diligent with training, particularly in the first two years of its life, you will reap the rewards of a well-behaved companion that is a joy to own. Remember, though, to be realistic in your expectations and prepare to forgive mistakes and celebrate achievements.

Left *Disciplining your dog is an essential means of asserting yourself as its leader and in maintaining a social order at home.*

EARLY TRAINING — GETTING IT RIGHT

The best way to discipline your dog is to enrol it in puppy preschool. Many veterinary practices are now running puppy preschools and these, if well managed, are invaluable because they allow puppies to socialize with other puppies and people, and they enable you to start training your dog from as early as seven weeks of age.

A good puppy preschool should not be a free-for-all with large numbers of uncontrolled puppies and children nor should it be a boring, regimented military camp. It should, wherever possible, combine supervised off-lead socialization with short periods of individual instruction on basic training. As the class progresses, the training should also be practised in a group situation.

Above *Puppy preschool is an excellent starting point for training.*
Below *Dogs and owners can make new friends every time they meet at the training school.*

REWARD-BASED TRAINING — POSITIVE REINFORCEMENT

Training should be based on positive reinforcement, not punishment. Reward-based training using food treats is, in my opinion, the best way to train puppies as they are very food-oriented at this stage in their life and are open to learning new things.

In reward-based training, the puppy receives a food treat the moment it performs a desirable behaviour. It is also praised verbally at the same time. For example, to teach a puppy to sit, a treat is held just in front of its nose and when it shows interest, the treat is moved up and backwards so that in reaching up and back for the treat, the puppy automatically sits. The 'sit' command is given at this time and when the puppy achieves the position, the treat is released and the puppy is verbally praised. Using this technique, puppies learn to sit happily on command very quickly, sometimes within minutes!

Stay away from classes run by control freaks who physically force puppies to sit by pulling their necks up and pushing their bottoms down, or who get them to lie down by pulling their legs out from under them while pulling down on their collars. This is not acceptable in training. Physically forcing puppies to behave in certain ways can be psychologically and sometimes physically damaging.

PUNISHMENT

Punishment is the use of an aversive stimulus in response to undesirable behaviour in order to decrease the likelihood of that particular action being repeated. If punishment is to be used, it must be appropriate in type and intensity, and must occur within seconds of the performance of the undesirable behaviour. It must also be followed by a command that enables an alternative action to be performed. For example, if your dog is jumping up at the bench to steal food and ignores the command 'no' followed by 'come', squirt him with a water pistol or use a foghorn to startle him. Then immediately ask him to sit, then to come and sit beside you. Reward his good behaviour with a pat. It is never acceptable to physically punish a dog by beating it.

Continue with your training after puppy school. Keep practising everything you have learned daily. If you are interested in agility or other areas of training, ask your veterinary surgeon to recommend a good training class. These classes usually start the puppies at six months of age.

Above *Your dog's training should always be based on reward and positive reinforcement.*

EQUIPMENT

There is a range of training aids and equipment available. Some of it is excellent while the rest is totally inappropriate.

The head collar

This is a wonderful training aid. It is similar to a horse halter, allowing your dog freedom to pant, drink and bark if it wants to while giving you full control of its head. The head collar is also designed to mimic the way a bitch controls her puppies by putting gentle pressure around the muzzle and behind the ears. Most dogs visibly relax and are more controlled when wearing a head collar.

Above Many veterinary surgeons recommend dogs wear a head collar, also known as a 'halti', as they cause no physical discomfort and guarantee a hassle-free walk.
Below Family walks will be a pleasure for everyone if your dog is fitted with a training aid.

Head collars should be correctly fitted. Your veterinary staff should be able to help you do this. It is usually a good idea to fit the head collar and take the dog straight out for a walk. Some dogs will paw at the collar when it is first put on and may rub their faces on the ground. They soon forget about it, however, and by the end of the walk are quite comfortable with the idea.

Choker chains

These have been used for years in training. They are based on negative reinforcement. If the dog pulls, the chain tightens and causes discomfort. If he stops pulling the discomfort goes away. Eventually, the sound of the chain slipping is enough to make the dog stop whatever he was about to do in anticipation of discomfort. The problem is that inexperienced people tend not to use the chain correctly and the dog does not learn to make the connection. The result is a dog pulling hard on a chain that is tightening around its neck. Chains used in this way can cause serious damage to the dog's airway.

Dogs should never be tied up in a choker as they can strangle themselves should they panic for some reason. Nor should they ever be held up in the air on the choker as is advocated by some trainers. This method, which was a cruel and potentially damaging UK army training method, is now discredited.

No-pull harnesses

These are designed to restrict the dog's forelimbs when it pulls. They are effective in some dogs. Usually they are used on dogs that cannot wear a head collar. It is important to check regularly for chafing under the forelegs.

Anti-bark/Training collars

Problem barking should always be assessed by a behaviourist. Never use any sort of anti-bark collar without expert advice. There are reasons why your dog barks and a suitable modification programme should be implemented. There are occasions where an anti-bark collar may be used temporarily as part of a behaviour- modification programme.

There are several types of anti-bark collar available: citronella collars that deliver a spray of citronella every time the dog barks, air-shot collars that deliver a blast of cold air rather than citronella and electric collars that deliver an electric shock.

In my opinion there is no place for electric dog collars in behavioural medicine. They are barbaric. Imagine how you would feel if you were to receive an electric shock each time you tried to speak.

Dogs are given no recourse to alternative behaviour. In fact, they are often left alone and unobserved during the day, wearing the corrective collar while their owners are at work. As a result, many of them end up as quivering wrecks, hiding under beds and shaking when their owners arrive home because they do not understand what is happening to them. These symptoms are exacerbated for dogs suffering from anxiety-based disorders.

Remote-controlled electric collars are used by some trainers to control dogs that chase livestock or cars. They should only be used by an experienced person, and then only in extreme circumstances, however, there's no guarantee that the dog won't revert to its former behaviour

when it is out of sight or not wearing the collar. The best prevention is to deny your dog access to livestock.

Citronella collars, although less severe than electric collars, can be damaging to dogs suffering from anxiety-based disorders. These collars deliver a spray of citronella into the dog's face whenever it barks. Some dogs become nauseated and vomit, others learn to ignore the spray and yet others stop barking while wearing the collar, but soon start again when it is removed.

Air-shot collars automatically emit a short jet of very cold gas in response to a loud bark. The sudden release of this gas causes an unpleasant mild to severe tactile sensation under the dog's chin and a hissing noise that momentarily startles it. These collars can also be operated by remote control, which makes them useful in modifying car chasing behaviour.

Above *A harness can be helpful when walking dogs, however, some dogs will insist on pulling hard against it. For this reason it is important to check for chafing in this area to ensure your dog is not experiencing any discomfort.*

TRAINING MYTHS AND LEGENDS

'Will using rewards make my dog constantly look for food?'

Owners are often worried that if they use reward-based training for puppies, they are encouraging them only to behave well within sight of food. This is not true. Reward-based training begins with rewarding the desired behaviour every time it occurs and connecting the command to the behaviour.

Verbal praise is also given with a food reward. Once the behaviour has been learned, the food rewards are given intermittently and finally can be phased out entirely if you wish. This is because your verbal praise is automatically associated with the food reward and becomes an adequate reward in itself. Simply put, the food is a primary reinforcement and your voice a secondary reinforcement.

Above *Giving a dog food rewards in return for good behaviour is the basis of reward-based training.*

'Should a biting puppy be punished with an Alpha Roll?'

This is an excessive training method that has been shown to be nothing more than a pointless act of cruelty. It involves grabbing the puppy and holding it on its back while staring directly into its eyes, until it stops wriggling and crying and gives up. Trainers will tell you that this is how bitches deal with naughty puppies. This is not true. Bitches don't have the hands to physically inflict this on the puppy.

This sort of treatment can either make the puppy scared of its owner or more aggressive. People who do this to adult dogs to assert their dominance are in serious danger of being badly bitten. Biting in puppies should be redirected to a toy and/or the time-out method used as described on p35.

'Does my dog know when he has done wrong, because when I come home he looks really guilty and I think he expects to be punished?'

Studies have proven that dogs do not remember having done something wrong earlier in the day as their association span between the 'crime' and the corrective measure is less than three seconds. The dog that has soiled the carpet or chewed a piece of furniture does not think to itself 'Oh no, here comes Mum. I'm really going to be in trouble for making a mess.'

It will not make any association with what it has done earlier in the day and your reaction on finding the mess. It will not understand why you are pointing and yelling, but will slink away in response to your body language, confused and upset by your behaviour. There is no point in punishing a dog in this situation.

WHO TO CONTACT IF YOU HAVE PROBLEMS

If you are experiencing behavioural problems with your puppy or dog, ask your veterinary surgeon to recommend someone who can help you. The options are varied, a good trainer, an animal behaviourist, or a veterinary animal behaviourist, depending on the type and severity of your problem.

TRAINERS

Trainers are those who run dog-obedience schools. Some of these people have certificates in dog training from recognized training schools using modern approved methods.

However, there are many people who have set up as trainers with little or no formal qualification, and others who are still using obsolete training methods based on punishment. Make sure you approach an approved trainer. Bear in mind, though, that although they can address your dog's unruly behaviour, they are not equipped to advise on aggression and barking, and are not qualified to deal with anxiety-based disorders.

ANIMAL BEHAVIOURISTS

These experts have science degrees in behavioural zoology or behavioural science. They have an understanding of animal psychology and development and can assess and advise on behavioural problems. They are not veterinary surgeons and are not licensed to prescribe medication, rather they resemble psychologists in human medicine.

VETERINARY ANIMAL BEHAVIOURISTS

Experts with a veterinary degree and further qualifications in the field of animal behaviour, are fully versed in the use of medication with behavioural modification and have in-depth knowledge of neurophysiology.

Veterinary animal behaviourists are qualified to assess whether an animal is neurologically abnormal and are able to prescribe appropriate treatment if it is. They are the equivalent of human psychiatrists.

Above *Veterinary surgeons are your first source of information should you be looking for the expertise of a trainer, animal behaviourist or veterinary animal behaviourist.*

Fears & Phobias

Fear is a normal response shown by dogs faced with the threat of injury or death. The fight/flight response that is triggered by fear-provoking stimuli is an important survival tactic: a dog that is attacked will experience a surge of adrenaline – an excitatory neurotransmitter – into the bloodstream. This will increase its heart rate and pace of breathing, helping it to run fast and react quickly. The hormone cortisol is also released into its system and this triggers the release of glucose, providing it with energy. Phobias, on the other hand, are debilitating. Abnormal responses to certain stimuli, that are immediate and excessively fearful, can be the result of a variety of environmental and genetic factors. Thunderstorms and fireworks are two of the most common forms. Animals suffering from phobias need medication, and their fearful responses can be reduced to a manageable level.

Left *Your unconditional love and support goes a long way to helping your dog cope with any anxiety it may be experiencing.*

Every time an animal experiences fear, a fear memory is created and this will be triggered the next time the animal is exposed to an equivalent stimulus.

This is obviously a useful thing if the previous response to that stimulus is remembered and it helps the animal to avoid danger in the future, but it can also be counter-productive when the fear is unfounded. For example, in a domestic situation it would be very useful if a dog that was hit by a car never again crossed the road on its own. It would be less useful if, as a result of the accident, the dog

Below *This dog is extremely fearful of getting in the car, as it triggers a fear memory in which he associates the vehicle with a traumatic car accident in the past.*

became terrified of roads and cars and as a result, could not be walked or transported anywhere.

Most animals can cope with fear, and with time, can learn to overcome it. For example, if a dog jumps up at a door which collapses, and the dog is hurt, it is unlikely to repeat the behaviour in the near future. However, if later on, its owner stands behind the door with a plate of tasty morsels and asks the dog to push through to get the food, it is likely to tentatively do so. If the door does not collapse this time and the food is enjoyable, the dog will become much less fearful of passing through the doorway again.

Just like people, some dogs are genetically more timid than others. These dogs take long to approach novel stimuli and strangers and are highly sensitive to sudden loud noises. If your puppy seems to be timid, try to gradually

expose it to as many positive novel situations in the first six months of its life. Use food rewards to make new experiences positive. Build up this regimen gradually.

Take the puppy to visit friends first, then to local shopping areas on quiet days, then on busy days, and then to more major shopping areas. Note that puppies have a fear-imprint period that endures between eight and 10 weeks of age and again at 16 weeks. It is important to avoid traumatic experiences at these times because fear memories created during these phases are very difficult to erase. As already discussed, when dogs show extreme, abnormal, fearful responses, often towards specific stimuli such as thunderstorms or fireworks, these animals are suffering from phobia which need to be treated.

THUNDERSTORM PHOBIA

As a storm builds animals that suffer from thunderstorm phobia become increasingly uneasy and at the height of the storm they reach a state of panic. In this mindset they can seriously damage themselves, as was the case with Tip, a two-year-old Labrador/Border Collie cross.

Above *Some dogs are terrified of thunderstorms and may exhibit symptoms of anxiety hours before they start, in direct response to a drop in barometric pressure.*

Tip pushed himself further behind the couch, his body shaking uncontrollably. With every crack of thunder he jumped and whimpered, then shook even more. Another vicious flash of lightning lit the room followed rapidly by a massive thunderclap.

Tip bolted from behind the couch and in his panic hit the glass door; the glass shattered and Tip ran out of the garden and down the road. All he could do was run, oblivious of his surroundings and of the blood running down his leg. Finally, when he could run no further, Tip sought refuge under a bush, whimpering.

Tip was found the next morning by a jogger, weak, exhausted and with a deep gash to his shoulder as well as several other less severe cuts. He was treated at the local veterinary clinic and returned to his distraught owner. This gentle dog suffered from thunderstorm phobia.

Tip's owner contacted a veterinary surgeon who prescribed anti-anxiety medication, which increases the amount of relaxing

neurochemicals in his brain to help reduce his anxiety. Tip is now medicated over the winter months and has additional medication during thunderstorms. To be effective, the additional medication is given at the first evidence of a drop in barometric pressure and repeated six hourly. Tip is still uneasy but his anxiety no longer escalates to panic.

Some dogs benefit from being calmly but firmly held during the thunder, however, it is best not to fuss too much or the fearful behaviour may be encouraged. It can also help to soundproof a room and have thick curtains at the windows to dull the sound of the thunder. A radio or television may help act as a distraction in some cases. If the dog wants to hide, allow it to. In fact, providing it with a cubby into which it may escape is a good idea.

Once on medication, if you want to desensitize your dog to sounds of thunderstorms and/or fireworks, you may want to expose it to low-level recordings of these which are available commercially. Reward your dog for calm behaviour. Gradually over a period of weeks, increase the volume of the recording until your dog no longer reacts to these loud sounds.

This can work well for other noise phobias as well. Nevertheless, despite these prescriptive methods in the case of thunderstorm phobia, it is impossible to mimic the factors present in a barometric pressure drop that seem to be major triggers in thunderstorm phobia.

NOISE PHOBIA

Dogs can develop a phobia to a sound that is specific to a particular thing or situation. Besides the fear associated with fireworks, triggers include the bustle of

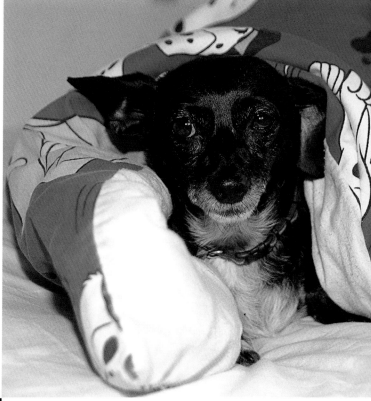

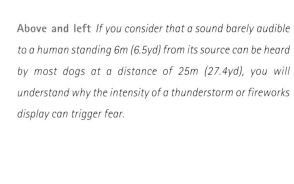

Above and left *If you consider that a sound barely audible to a human standing 6m (6.5yd) from its source can be heard by most dogs at a distance of 25m (27.4yd), you will understand why the intensity of a thunderstorm or fireworks display can trigger fear.*

traffic, especially revving motorbikes or cars backfiring; noise from building sites, especially staple guns and skill saws, and sometimes sound from jet aircraft or helicopters.

Dogs suffering from this condition usually shake and tremble when exposed to the specific noise they fear and will try to hide. If they are confined close to its source, they are likely to become frenetic in their attempts to escape.

There is evidence for genetic predisposition in dogs to noise phobia; they need medication, a behaviour-modification programme that involves desensitization and counterconditioning, and are taught to relax and perform another behaviour in the face of the stimulus that triggers the phobic response.

There is a similarity in a dog's behaviour towards noise phobia and separation anxiety. In both conditions, dogs try desperately to escape from confined spaces, sometimes hurting themselves in the process. As a result, owners can mistake the one condition for the other. Expert assessment is required. The case of Sammy a 12-year-old Golden Retriever, is a good example of this.

Sammy was presented to the behaviour clinic as a possible case of separation anxiety, with a recent history of trying to tear his way out of the garden through a solid wooden fence. His feet and gums were damaged and he had dug up most of his owner's carefully landscaped garden.

He had never behaved in such a manner prior to this and seemed to be getting worse by the weeks. The owner had recently moved from a rural property, and the house to which the family relocated was on a main road, surrounded by a 2m (2.1yd) fence.

Sammy lived with his sister Greta. During the day, both dogs were left in the garden. There was a porch in which they could sleep, a paddling pool to play in and lots of toys. They were well exercised daily. If it rained, the dogs were left inside.

Sammy was relaxed about his owner moving from room to room and didn't necessarily follow him. He was fine on rainy days when left inside, never making any attempts at escape. However, on fine days he seemed reluctant to stay in the yard and paced nervously while his owner was preparing to leave.

Below *Gradually exposing dogs to recordings of sounds they fear is a way of desensitizing them to their phobia.*

Video footage showed that both dogs settled after the owner had left. They lay side by side in the sun for about 15 minutes. Then several large trucks rattled past, and both dogs became restless and disturbed, pacing around the garden. A group of motorbikes followed and Sammy started to paw at the gate. A car backfired and both dogs jumped. Sammy began to scour the perimeter fence for a means of escape.

The owner said that Sammy hated fireworks. He was also disturbed by road noise. He had nowhere to go to avoid it. Gradually his anxiety increased until he felt desperate to escape.

Sammy was put on anti-anxiety medication and provided with a dog door into the garage area. After two weeks he was much more settled and relaxed about being in the new environment. He had started a desensitization protocol, designed to teach him to relax and concentrate on his owner in return for food while a recording of various noises was played. The volume of the recording was to be gradually increased until he was able to remain relaxed in the presence of noises that he had previously found distressing. He was coping well with the first stages of the programme. However, two months into therapy, his owner moved house to a cul-de-sac in a quiet area with a bush park at the back. Sammy was gradually weaned off the medication and was perfectly happy from then on.

This case emphasizes the need for dogs that are noise sensitive to have somewhere to escape. Soundproofing a downstairs room or even a garden shed, and providing access by means of a dog door can be very helpful to animals that find traffic noise disturbing. Noise-phobic animals can be desensitized using exposure to noise recordings at gradually increasing volumes. They must be on

Above *Although cars are our most reliable means of transportation, and we cannot imagine our lives without them, we tend to forget that they are also the cause of much fear in our dogs due to the loud noises they make.*
Left *A dog needs to feel secure when left home alone, and a dog door allowing him into your house is the ideal solution, so that he can escape perceived threats.*

anti-anxiety medication while this is done and they should be taught how to relax in the presence of the noise triggers. Forcibly exposing the dogs to increasing levels of noise without using medication and relaxation techniques is likely to exacerbate the condition.

SPECIFIC AND SITUATIONAL PHOBIAS

Dogs may develop phobias of specific situations or stimuli, such as in the case of agoraphobia, a fear of open spaces. One of the most common phobias is the veterinary clinic. Some dogs begin to shake as soon as the car pulls up in front of the clinic, and they remain stressed and anxious throughout their visit, despite attempts to make their stay pleasant.

Specific phobias may include certain people, such as tall men, or they may include specific objects such as bikes or skateboards. Dogs most likely to develop phobias include reactive breeds such as Border Collies and German Shepherds, those that have had very limited exposure to stimuli in early life and those that have been in animal shelters.

Phobias may result from traumatic experiences. Often dogs that have been hurt in road-traffic accidents while passengers in a car may show extreme anxiety if asked to get into a car again. In other cases, there is no obvious reason for the animal to be afraid at all.

Make a point of not reinforcing an inappropriate fear-response in your dog. Telling him that it's okay when he shakes and trembles and tries to scrabble off the examination table at the veterinary clinic reinforces the fearful behaviour. It is best to tell him 'no', 'sit' and 'stay', and to praise him only when he is calm. This applies to any situation where an inappropriate fear-response is shown in your dog.

Above *Taking in his environment, this dog uses a leafy enclosure in the garden as a means to observe the outside world while remaining hidden himself.*

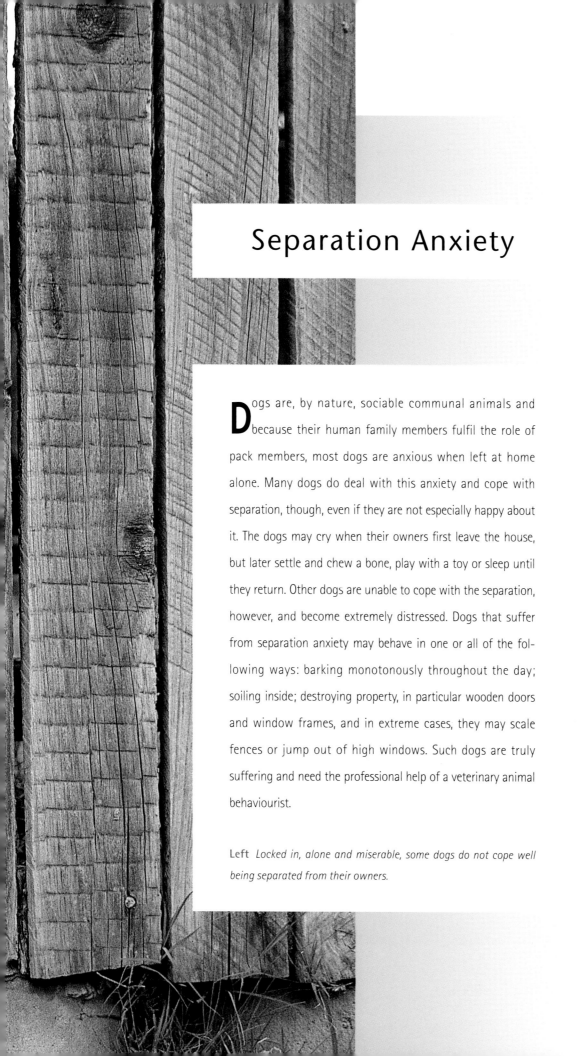

Separation Anxiety

Dogs are, by nature, sociable communal animals and because their human family members fulfil the role of pack members, most dogs are anxious when left at home alone. Many dogs do deal with this anxiety and cope with separation, though, even if they are not especially happy about it. The dogs may cry when their owners first leave the house, but later settle and chew a bone, play with a toy or sleep until they return. Other dogs are unable to cope with the separation, however, and become extremely distressed. Dogs that suffer from separation anxiety may behave in one or all of the following ways: barking monotonously throughout the day; soiling inside; destroying property, in particular wooden doors and window frames, and in extreme cases, they may scale fences or jump out of high windows. Such dogs are truly suffering and need the professional help of a veterinary animal behaviourist.

Left *Locked in, alone and miserable, some dogs do not cope well being separated from their owners.*

SEPARATION ANXIETY

Zac's behaviour is typical of separation anxiety, and many dogs like him will respond similarly to being left home alone because they lack the neurochemicals to help them deal with the anxiety this causes.

Zac paced and whined, licking his lips. As his owner Dianne reached for her coat he began to tremble. Telling him not to be silly, Dianne gave him a biscuit and left.

Zac dropped the biscuit and ran to the window, watching the car move down the drive. He began to bark, frantically running between the front door and the window. He scrabbled at the doorframe and tore at the mat. Finally with claws bleeding and paws full of splinters he curled up on the sofa, every 10 minutes or so emitting a sad, monotonous bark.

Dianne returned to find the hall trashed and Zac covered in blood. He was thrilled to see her and bounced about despite his sore feet. He raced to the biscuit she'd given him in the morning and ate it. This was the worst he'd been. She'd returned home on occasion to find a favourite cushion chewed, but she'd assumed he had been amusing himself and had bought him more toys.

The 18-month-old Golden Retriever had always been clingy while Dianne was at home and had cried whenever she left, even though her partner was usually home while she was out. Over the last two weeks though, her partner had been away overseas and Zac was not coping with being alone. Dianne had his feet treated at her local veterinary surgeon and he was referred to a behaviour clinic where he was put on anti-anxiety medication and a behaviour-modification programme. Dianne took two weeks off work to begin his therapy and her partner continued with it when he returned from his overseas trip. Zac was kept on his medication for four months and then weaned off it over two weeks. He is now able to stay at home on his own, without the former anxiety, although his owners ensure he is never alone for more than four hours.

Separation anxiety is often treated with medication to reduce a dog's apprehension, and the animal is then put on a behaviour-modification programme, which desensitizes it to the separation process from its owners and teaches it to relax when alone. Such dogs are too anxious to learn without medication and often cause serious damage to themselves and their property.

This destructive damage, which results from the dog's attempt to get to its owners, usually

Left *Unable to cope with the silence and isolation at home, this dog lies miserably awaiting his owner's return.*

Left *This dog watches his owners' departure intently. Facing another day on his own, lonely and insecure, he may stand at this watchpoint until they return.*

begins in the first 30 minutes after they leave their homes. It is really important not to punish your dog for any damage it may have caused in your absence, though.

Some dogs can cope better if they have another dog for company during the day, but for many, this makes no difference. They want the members of their 'pack' at home where they belong.

Sometimes they are concerned about the absence of one particular member and will continue to show anxiety until that person returns home, no matter who else is present.

Separation anxiety may occur in dogs that previously seemed to cope with separation if there has been a period during which their owners were constantly at home, for example, during a prolonged illness or even a holiday, or in some cases when a work timetable suddenly changes.

Some owners are unaware that their dog is suffering from separation anxiety in the daytime until their neighbours start to complain about constant barking and excessive howling or until they see signs of destruction.

If your dog does these things, consider leaving a video tape recorder running in his area during the day to see exactly what he does when you leave. The videotape can then be carefully analyzed by your veterinary animal behaviourist.

Clues that your dog may be anxious about being alone include:

- Following you from room to room while you prepare to leave.
- Pacing and salivating.
- Trembling.
- Yawning and lip licking.
- Placing itself between you and the exit, and pawing at you.
- Not eating its breakfast or meals during the day, then immediately eating the food that it has left untouched as soon as you arrive home.
- Crying as you depart.

Above *Sometimes the daytime company of another dog can prevent separation anxiety while you're at work.*

PREVENTING SEPARATION ANXIETY

To a large extent, whether or not your dog will suffer from separation anxiety is genetically determined. However, there are things you can do to decrease the severity of the condition and to prevent it developing in borderline dogs.

When you get a puppy, accustom it to spending some time alone during the day. Provide a bed and a stuffed toy within a crate or small confined area of the house so that the puppy can feel secure (see p36).

As your dog grows older, train it to stay on its bed sometimes when you are busy in other parts of the house. Reward it when you return with a food treat and a pat.

Make sure your dog is well exercised before you leave for work in the morning. A good 30-minute run is necessary for most dogs, exercise helps to relax your dog. Also vary your morning routine.

Most people seem to develop a predictable morning ritual. Try to avoid this and vary the sequence of coffee, shower and breakfast everyday. Play with your car keys sometimes when you are at home and settled for the evening. The distinct jangle of car keys is an instant signal to most dogs that your departure is imminent, one which is set to change if you do this.

If your friend also has a dog that must be home alone for a time during the day, it may be a good idea for your two dogs to stay together at either her home or yours. In this way, the dogs can keep each other company, while you are free to do what you need to do.

are away for an extended period. It is a good idea to leave a familiar toy or bedding with the dog.

There are alternatives to kennels for those dogs finding the experience traumatic. Employing a housesitter works for some dog owners. If dogs are socialized with the sitters first, and then left in their own home environment with them, many of these dogs cope very well.

Developing an 'aunty' system with friends who also have dogs or other animals is useful. The dogs become familiar with the other homes and are relaxed if left there. They miss their owners but seem to cope well in most cases.

If something unforeseen happens in your life that requires you to suddenly put your dog in kennels, it may be worth giving it anti-anxiety medication to cope with the situation should it suffer from separation anxiety. Discuss this with your veterinary surgeon.

DOGS LEFT IN KENNELS

Going to boarding kennels can be a traumatic experience for some dogs and can trigger separation anxiety if not handled appropriately. Older dogs that spend most of their time with their owners are most at risk. These dogs can suffer severe distress when suddenly placed in a kennel. They may refuse to eat and spend their time clinging to familiar bedding or perhaps their lead, shaking and trembling. They may bark and sometimes try desperately to dig or chew their way out of their confines. When they eventually go home, many dogs are terrified of being left alone and will show separation anxiety from then on.

If you think it is likely that your dog may need to go into kennels at any stage, find an establishment where the people are happy for you to visit regularly with your dog before you go away. This allows your dog to become familiar with the surroundings and the staff. If the owners of the boarding kennel have their own dog, encourage your dog to play and establish a rapport with it.

Try to visit weekly for one month, then leave your dog overnight and see how it copes. Do this weekly for a month, and if all is well, you should be able to leave the dog while you

Above Try to accustom your dog to kennels gradually. Make short regular visits for any length of time, so that he is not suddenly abandoned in a strange place.
Below If you do not like the idea of housing your dog in a kennel while you are away on holiday, why not employ the services of a dogsitter?

Obsessive-compulsive Disorder

Obsessive-compulsive disorder presents itself as repetitive behaviour with no apparent purpose. It interferes with a dog's normal routine; examples of it include tail chasing, fly biting (snapping at imaginary flies), foot chewing, fence running, shadow chasing and digging. A neurological disorder, obsessive-compulsive behaviour may debilitate dogs because they find it difficult to stop even to eat. They are so determined to continue with their single-minded behaviour that they actively resist any attempt to be removed from the situation. In the case of tail chasing, dogs may bite and seriously damage their tails. Those that dig compulsively often tear their feet until they bleed, oblivious to the pain. Fence runners wear in paths through the garden where they habitually run. Animals that exhibit this behaviour need to be medicated. They also need to be put on a behaviour-modification programme and exercised more.

Left *Tail chasing is a relatively common obsessive-compulsive disorder. Affected dogs may cause themselves serious damage.*

If your dog is showing bizarre behaviour, take it to your veterinary surgeon to have a full clinical examination and blood test done. If the results are normal, he will probably be referred to a veterinary animal behaviourist who will assess your dog's behaviour and advise you accordingly.

To this end, the behaviourist will determine whether or not the dog can be distracted from the behaviour, and will assess the situations in which the behaviour occurs. For example, the dog that tail chases when you have guests but not when you are free to give it your full attention is probably attention seeking. If it stops the behaviour as soon as you pick it up, put on its lead or appear with a food bowl, it is very likely that the behaviour is attention seeking rather than obsessive compulsive.

Roxy, a three-year-old Rottweiler, was obsessed with shadows. She would stare fixedly at the gently moving shadow of a tree branch on the lawn. Every so often she would bark, then she would stare transfixed, seemingly unable to move.

Above *This Bull Terrier attacks his tyre obsessively, causing himself severe oral injury. Fortunately, in this case the solution is simple: the toy can be removed.*
Right *Repeatedly staring and barking at his own shadow, this German Shepherd has little time for anything else, including interacting with his owners.*

Should you suspect that your dog is suffering from obsessive-compulsive disorder, it is very important that his condition be properly diagnosed and treated. Some behaviour may appear to be obsessive compulsive but it may in fact be a form of attention seeking or it may be due to some other medical disorder such as a brain tumour or localized disease.

Some dogs may exhibit more than one obsessive-compulsive behavioural trait and may have other behavioural disorders as well. A case I observed at a colleague's referral practice a few years ago is a good example.

Fran was a two-year-old Bull Terrier bitch belonging to a young couple. Fran was a very pretty Bull Terrier with unusually large ears and attractive markings. She was generally very friendly to strangers but had begun to terrify her owners with her bizarre behaviour.

The couple had a ceiling fan in their bedroom, and recently Fran had become obsessed with it. She would race into the bedroom, jump on the bed and bark at the fan. She had bitten the young man when he attempted to stop this behaviour. Fran had also become fixated on the water in the shower and would sit staring at the drops. If she was disturbed in any way, even by someone walking past, she became agitated.

If Roxy's owners called her, she looked briefly in their direction, then returned to her staring. If Roxy's owners tried to put her lead on and remove her from the lawn, she would resist and even bite them. When they did manage to move her away, she seemed distracted. As soon as she was released she would return to her shadows. Roxy was suffering from obsessive-compulsive disorder. In this case it was important to prevent her sighting the shadow on the lawn during her initial stage of therapy, and then to teach her an alternative behaviour in the presence of this trigger.

The neurological abnormalities that cause obsessive-compulsive disorder, as in Roxy's case, have been shown to be inherited, so animals showing this behaviour should not have pups. Such obsessive behaviour is very common in Bull Terriers and Cavalier King Charles Spaniels. Bull terriers are known for tail chasing and spaniels for fly biting.

Above left *Tail chasing is a common obsessive-compulsive disorder in Bull Terriers.*
Above *A dog fly biting (snapping at imaginary flies) may seem funny at first, but when this action is performed repeatedly it can become an incredibly annoying pastime.*

Fran had also started growling at the young lady in doorways and around food. She had attacked her for no apparent reason on two occasions. These attacks were so severe that the lady had shut herself in her room and called her husband to come home.

This dog was showing obsessive-compulsive disorder and dominance aggression. She was medicated and her owners were given a protocol to follow. After two weeks, however, the owners decided to euthanase the dog. They couldn't cope with the strain. The young lady had lost confidence in the dog and both partners were very stressed.

This case serves to demonstrate how serious these problems can be. It is very important to seek help early, as soon as you notice your dog's bizarre behaviour. Fence running, for example, can be particularly detrimental to a dog's health because it is so energy expendable and because dogs exhibiting this behaviour are often so agitated that they really don't eat much.

Above *Distracting your dog from its obsessive behaviour with the promise of food is one way of refocusing its attention away from the object on which it was fixated.*

Below *Dogs can become fixated on a particular object such as a favourite toy. Do not encourage this behaviour, preferably take it away from your dog during playtime.*

Anna, a three-year-old Rough-coated Collie presented with a history of barking and fence running. She was underweight, hardly ate and was always on the go, circling the dining-room table incessantly while her owners sat talking to visitors, and barking and running circuits around the house when the neighbours drove or walked alongside the fence.

When let outside she would run in a figure-of-eight along the fence, around the house and back again, barking. She did not return when called. There was a track worn in the ground where Anna ran along the same route.

The Collie was placed on anti-anxiety medication for her mental condition after blood tests and clinical evaluations proved that, despite being underweight, her kidneys and liver were functioning normally. She was also placed on a behaviour-modification programme to teach her to relax and ignore sensory stimuli. After two weeks she was eating normally but was still hyper-reactive and constantly running around the house. Over two months, the abnormal behaviour had decreased by 50 per cent and the dog had gained weight. She was still a little over-reactive to stimuli. After four months Anna was behaving normally. Her medication was reduced, but she began to show increased reactivity again.

It was decided then to maintain her at the previous dosage of medication. Anna has done well and is a much happier dog. She has blood tests as part of her routine annual health check to ensure that she is able to cope with continued medication and has had no problems. Her owners are much relieved and can relax and enjoy being dog owners.

Below *Fence running can be debilitating. Affected dogs may damage their feet, and often lose large amounts of weight as a result of their incessant activity because it so energy consuming. In addition, because they are so physically occupied, they do not remember to eat.*

Behavioural medicine

In behavioural medicine anti-anxiety medication is used to restore neurochemical balance in a dog's brain. Many of these drugs increase the levels of serotonin (a relaxing neurotransmitter) available to the brain. Some also decrease the amount of norepinephrine (an excitatory neurotransmitter) (see p21). Over time these drugs can cause the development of increased receptor sites in the brain for serotonin, thereby increasing the animal's ability to cope with anxiety. Some drugs can also promote nerve-cell production.

Medication is given to anxious animals during behaviour modification, allowing them to relax enough to learn alternative behaviours. Most animals are treated for four to six months but this depends on the severity of the condition. The drug is then gradually withdrawn. If permanent changes in neuroreceptors have been achieved and the modification programme has been successfully implemented, the animal may not need further medication. When some animals are not cured their medication needs to be continued.

Unfortunately obsessive-compulsive disorder results from complex neurological abnormalities and many animals need lifelong medication.

Aggression

Aggression is part of normal dog behaviour. It is observed between rivals fighting over territory or mates, in self-protection when the dog is threatened and when defending food or other prized resources. Aggression can, however, be excessive and inappropriate. As with all behaviour, some dogs are genetically more predisposed to aggression than others. Some breeds have been selectively bred to be aggressive towards other dogs so that they can be used for dog fighting, some are bred to act aggressively towards people, while others have been selected for extreme territorial aggression and are used as guard dogs. In very aggressive breeds, the majority of dogs may not react normally to signals of submission, may not signal their intent and may attack suddenly with no apparent provocation. Given that there are exceptions to the rule, any breed can be selected for traits of either aggression or timidity.

Left *Living with an excessively aggressive dog can be unnerving, particularly if you or your family are under constant threat of attack.*

Above *Selection for physical traits in dogs may lead to the unintentional selection of an aggressive disposition.*

Breeders sometimes select for physical traits only and do not consider temperament. This increases their chances of producing animals that tend towards dominance or fear-aggression. An example would be where breeders select dogs with high-set tails, a feature that goes hand-in-hand with a bold, aggressive temperament. Nevertheless, despite this tendency, the behaviour of the genetically aggressive dog can also be influenced positively or negatively by its environment and experience.

Dominance aggression

Dominance aggression in dogs is an extreme inappropriate form of aggression that is often directed towards members of a household and occurs because the dogs intend to control the family members.

This was the case with Adam, a three-year-old male Schnauzer whose aggression was directed towards Noel, the 14-year-old son of the family, whose life was made particularly difficult as a result.

Adam had reached the point where he would attack the boy on sight. He would wait at the door to Noel's room, ready to confront with him should he come out. Noel had to call out to his family to remove the dog if he wanted to go to another room in the house. Adam would bark continuously while the boy was out of his room.

Noel had three scars on his legs where Adam had bitten him severely enough to require stitches. Understandably, Noel was quite uncomfortable with the dog. Adam also resented having his collar put on and would snap at anyone who did this when he was not in the mood for it. He growled if asked to move when lying on the sofa and when approached while eating.

Adam is one of the worst cases of dominance aggression that I have seen. Obviously he represented a definite danger to the family, especially to Noel, so he was put straight onto medication and castration was strongly recommended, although the family elected not to castrate the dog. He was put onto a strict modification programme and was taught to walk in a head collar.

Noel was put in charge of feeding the dog and was to take over exercising him as well. At first, he had to do all of this while the dog was on a head collar and lead, held by another family member. He was also directed to undergo daily training sessions with the dog and a protocol was devised to desensitize Adam to Noel's movements in and out of his room.

Progress was slow as the boy was not particularly enamoured with the dog and gave up easily. However, with a lot of family support, progress was made and after six months the situation was more controlled.

Although Adam still barked at Noel sometimes, he was far less aggressive. Noel could sit comfortably in the lounge without risk and could safely leave and return to the lounge without being attacked. He could feed and walk the dog. Adam stopped growling at other family members over the issues previously mentioned. It took more than a year, though, before harmony was restored to the household.

Adam has had to stay on medication due to his condition. There are still issues with him when family members become too relaxed, but they know how to deal with them.

Above *Puppy play rarely leads to aggressive behaviour, however, this puppy is being a little overzealous and should not be allowed to play in this manner.*

Dogs require clear signals about their position in the hierarchy (social order) of the household. If they do not receive these signals, then at about 18 to 36 months (the age of social maturity) they will begin to test their boundaries and challenge family members, much as teenage children do. In some animals, this can include extreme aggression, and the family is at risk of great physical harm, particularly if there are children involved.

Challenges occur over various resources. Typically, the dog will start growling if asked to move off the sofa or it may guard a doorway and prevent anyone from entering. It may challenge the application of a lead or harness, or refuse to leave the car on request, biting anyone who attempts to remove it forcibly.

Dogs that are genetically dominant in nature will show the most severe signs. Some of these dogs are convinced of their supremacy, others are not quite sure and are seeking answers. The former group are the most difficult to cope with.

These dogs need a complete and radical change in handling. They are put on a strict behaviour-modification programme which involves earning all the attention they get, being allowed on furniture or beds only with their owners' permission and being required to perform deferent behaviours frequently throughout the day such as sitting, lying down and rolling over.

If the dogs represent an obvious danger to one or more family members, they are usually put on anti-anxiety medication which is also known to curb aggression. This allows the owners to remain safe during the behaviour-modification programme.

Often a dog will direct its aggression towards a member of the household which it perceives to be closest to itself in hierarchy. This is often a young member of the family. The case of Adam provides an excellent example of how severe this situation may become. It is interesting that three other dogs from the same kennels were treated for dominance aggression. All had the same sire. The others were less severe cases of aggression and were rectified without the use of medication.

Inter-dog aggression

This type of aggression generally refers to that exhibited by a dog towards another unfamiliar dog. It is common for one dog to take an apparent dislike to another while out walking, to posture and growl, and even to scuffle, ending with one of them in a submissive posture.

Above *It would be wise for the owner of this dog to move him on quickly to avoid a fight, in order to desensitize him to the presence of other dogs.*

There are dogs, however, that become aggressive at the first sight of another dog on the horizon, snarling, barking and straining at the lead to get to it. When released from the lead these dogs are likely to lunge straight at the oncoming dog without stopping to notice signals.

This behaviour may be fear-based or it may be that the dog is incapable of recognizing and responding normally to social signals. Fear-based inter-dog aggression is sometimes seen in dogs that have been attacked by street dogs without provocation while out walking and have become afraid of any dog they come into contact with.

It seems that rushing in to attack is a form of protection for such dogs and this behaviour is anxiety based which was the case with Archie, a four-year-old Blue Heeler whose fear of other dogs was reinforced by his owner's reactions.

Archie stopped short, head up and tail down, hair standing up on his neck and rump. A low growl rumbled from his throat and he quivered all over. As the Border Collie approached, Archie dropped into a crouch, and when the dog was near enough, he launched himself at it snarling and snapping.

His owner tugged frantically at the lead, shouting at him to stop, but Archie was oblivious. The Collie was quick and leapt sideways, avoiding the attack. At that moment its owner called and it returned obediently. Archie remained trembling and growling, his owner in tears, apologizing for his behaviour.

Archie was presented to the clinic for aggression towards other dogs while out walking. The aggression had begun after Archie was attacked and severely bitten by unaccompanied dogs three times in two weeks.

His owner was now terrified of meeting other dogs when out walking with him. For two weeks she had not dared leave her property; then steeling herself, she had begun to force herself to walk him, but did so in the very early morning in the hope of avoiding other dogs. If she saw dogs in the distance she would turn away immediately and run in the opposite direction in the hope of avoiding conflict.

Archie was put on a modification programme designed to teach him to relax and concentrate on his owner when in the presence of other dogs. Given that this situation would provoke fear and aggression in him, Archie was given anti-anxiety medication while on the programme which decreased his aggressive response in these circumstances. The medication enabled him to relax enough to learn and decrease the likelihood of a repeat aggressive reaction. Archie was also taught to walk in a head collar. It helped his owner feel confident that she had control while walking him. It was important for her to overcome her fear before she could help Archie overcome his.

The treatment worked well and now both owner and dog are relaxed and comfortable again in the presence of other dogs.

Dogs that show inter-dog aggression out of fear respond well to desensitization programmes where they are taught to relax and accept the controlled presence of other dogs. They are brought progressively closer over time and finally they are encouraged to play together. If a dog shows signs of extreme fear, it may need anti-anxiety medication for a short period of time to help it get over any negative effects from previous trauma and to enable it to learn to accept other dogs.

Some particularly aggressive dogs do not read signals given by other dogs and cannot socialize successfully. They are often extremely dominant, and tend to be worse on familiar territory, so much of their behaviour may be an extreme form of territorial aggression. The problem with many of these dogs is that they will severely injure other dogs. Often their attack is frenzied and they will continue to attack and sometimes kill, even if the other animal is in a completely submissive posture.

Dogs that are abnormal and show severe inter-dog aggression can be managed but usually cannot be cured of the behaviour. Such animals should be walked on head collars and taught to perform alternative behaviours when another dog appears. Medication that decreases extreme aggression is sometimes used.

Aggression towards familiar dogs

Aggression can occur between dogs in the same household. The most common presentation of this is where an older and younger dog live happily together until the younger dog reaches social maturity. At this age the younger dog may challenge the older dog for access to prized resources such as food, sleeping areas, or proximity to and attention from the owner. Usually, the older dog will put the younger one firmly in its place and the problem will be solved.

Left *Going to the beach with your dog can be an ordeal if it is inappropriately aggressive towards other dogs. Such behaviour should be evaluated by a veterinary animal behaviourist.*

maintained. One dog must be clearly dominant or they will continue to fight. Until this delineation is achieved, do not leave the two dogs alone together, as you are likely to return to a blood bath. In some cases where the situation cannot be resolved, it may be necessary to relocate one of the dogs.

If, however, the older dog is becoming frail, or the younger dog is of a larger and stronger body type, and has a more aggressive nature, the younger dog may push the issue until the older one gives in. If the older dog resists, it may be seriously hurt or, in extreme cases, killed.

The way to deal with this situation is to reinforce the dominant position of the dog most likely to succeed in a fight. If the younger dog is bigger, stronger and dominant in nature, then, although you will feel terrible doing this, you need to reinforce it as the top dog. So feed it first, greet it first, and allow it priority access to everything.

If the older dog is still strong and prepared to dominate and is fit enough to succeed, then support the older dog and actively discourage the younger one from challenging it.

The main thing here is that you need to make sure that a clear hierarchy is

Above *Predatory aggression in dogs is often most apparent on farms where they target the small, vulnerable animals.*

Predatory aggression

Dogs are, by their very nature, predators. Some have a stronger predatory instinct than others and, as a result, can be difficult to keep in suburban or rural areas. They are considered abnormal in that their predatory drive is excessive compared with most pet dogs. Those dogs that have very little predatory drive will mother and protect anything small and furry.

Dogs that show extreme predatory aggression typically kill vulnerable, furry animals on sight. Pet rabbits, guinea pigs, chickens and cats are all fair game. In rural areas, sheep and young calves or deer may be targeted. Such dogs must be denied access to livestock. It is not possible, no matter how well trained they are, to guarantee that these dogs will not kill if they are left alone with prey animals or cats. Dogs with a strong predatory drive tend to be silent stalkers. They eye their prey, then stalk, kill and eat it.

Predatory aggression is neurologically different in origin from fear aggression, dominance aggression and inter-dog aggression, and as a result, does not respond to medication. These animals must be kept away from children. Babies and toddlers behave in a manner similar to prey. They cry, squeal and move erratically and can trigger this predatory behaviour with tragic results. Any child younger than seven should never be left unsupervised with any dog.

Idiopathic aggression

Idiopathic aggression can be defined as a form of abnormal aggression with an unknown cause. Dogs that have this condition have aggressive bouts with an almost seizure-like quality. Their eyes become glazed and owners describe them as possessed. Lifelong medication is necessary, and even when medicated, some dogs will have aggressive incidents, although less violent. Most owners elect euthanasia, such as was the case with Sam.

Sam stood on the landing snarling and barking, saliva dripping from his mouth, pupils dilated. Horrified, his young owner, who had just returned from a party at two o'clock in the morning, backed off and closed the door to the entrance. Hearing the commotion, the rest of the family appeared at the top of the stairs. Sam turned towards them growling. The lady of the house tried to approach him, speaking softly. Sam lunged at her, lost his footing and tumbled to the foot of the stairs. He picked himself up and continued to bark, drooling, pupils dilated.

Sam's owners called me. When I arrived, Sam was still lunging and growling. The man of the house grabbed the muzzle I had brought and, despite my warning, approached Sam to apply the muzzle. Sam bit through his arm. The man flung himself backward to safety and I bandaged his arm. I had also brought a catching pole (a long pole with a slip noose), so while someone distracted the dog, I passed the pole through the front door, slipping the noose over his head. Passing the pole to the boy, I ran to the other door and administered a strong sedative.

I took Sam to the clinic. When he recovered from sedation he was disoriented but no longer vicious. Blood tests were unremarkable. Three weeks later, Sam did it again. This time his owners opted for euthanasia. A post-mortem examination revealed no physical cause for his behaviour.

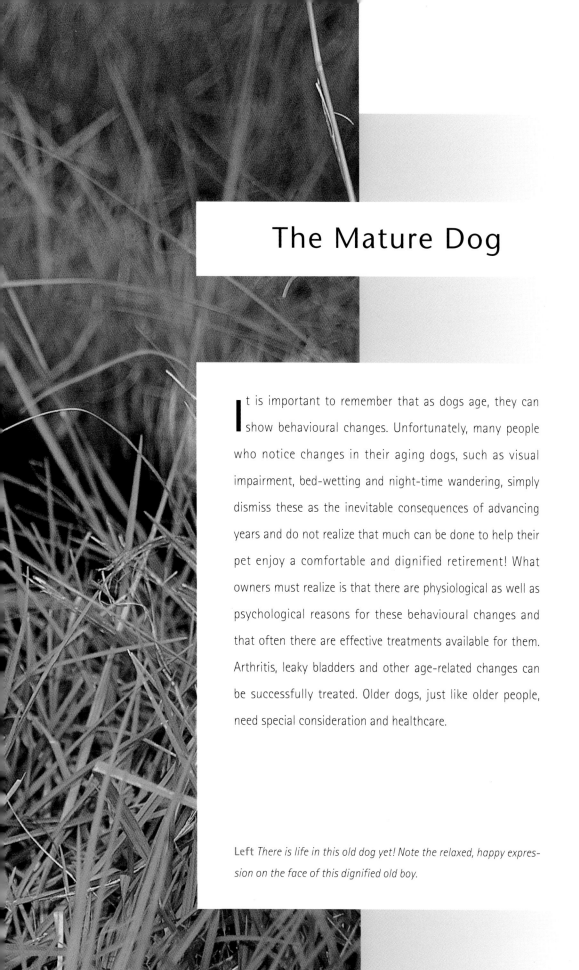

The Mature Dog

It is important to remember that as dogs age, they can show behavioural changes. Unfortunately, many people who notice changes in their aging dogs, such as visual impairment, bed-wetting and night-time wandering, simply dismiss these as the inevitable consequences of advancing years and do not realize that much can be done to help their pet enjoy a comfortable and dignified retirement! What owners must realize is that there are physiological as well as psychological reasons for these behavioural changes and that often there are effective treatments available for them. Arthritis, leaky bladders and other age-related changes can be successfully treated. Older dogs, just like older people, need special consideration and healthcare.

Left *There is life in this old dog yet! Note the relaxed, happy expression on the face of this dignified old boy.*

Canine Cognitive Dysfunction

Canine Cognitive Dysfunction is an age-related mental degeneration in dogs which is the equivalent of Alzheimer's disease in humans. Affected animals suffer from a lack of dopamine (a neurotransmitter) and parts of their brains are destroyed by the deposition of a substance called amyloid.

Affected animals seem disoriented at times and often bark for no reason. They wander into corners, ask for food and then forget to eat it, and sometimes start soiling inside. They often become very insecure and show signs of separation anxiety.

The good news is that there are drugs to treat this condition. Some work by causing vasodilation, increasing blood supply to the brain, thereby increasing oxygen and glucose availability. These drugs may be helpful if administered early in a dog's aging process. Others increase dopamine levels in the brain and are neuroprotective.

Below *Old dogs may suffer a condition similar to Alzheimer's disease in people. Afflicted animals often look vacant and spend time staring into space. This condition can be treated if caught early.*

Gus wandered out stiffly into the courtyard and stood staring into the distance. After five minutes, he turned and walked up to the wall surrounding the garden, where he stood unsure of where to go next, apparently having lost his bearings. Gus's owner Sylvia noticed him from the kitchen window and went outside to him and gently led him back inside.

She had just spent most of the night getting out of bed to see what was wrong with him as he paced up and down the hall. Twice she had let him out into the garden and he had stood looking vacant for a while and then wandered back inside.

Sometimes Gus would stop in the middle of eating and stare into space for five minutes. Twice in the last month, he had seemed confused about where the floor ended and the yard began and had soiled on the hall floor. Sylvia had recently begun to consider having Gus put to sleep because at times he seemed to have very little quality of life.

It was a hard decision because at the age of 14, this lovely old Golden Retriever was still physically fit apart from slight arthritis in his left hip, which was medically managed. He still had some good days, when he seemed totally normal and aware of everything around him.

After a complete medical examination and blood profile, Gus was put onto medication known as selegiline hydrochloride which has multiple benefits. This drug is also used to treat Alzheimer's disease in humans, it increases dopamine and reduces the number of oxygen-free radicals which are known to damage brain tissue. Within a month Gus's behaviour was radically changed. He slept through the night, was well aware of his surroundings, ate all his dinner immediately, and was playful and keen to go out for walks.

He still asked to go out and sometimes seemed to have forgotten what he wanted to do once he got there, but these episodes were much less frequent and shorter in duration.

Gus's condition is seen relatively commonly in older dogs. Medication, given in the early stages of the disease, can improve the dog's mental awareness and can prevent progression of the disease.

Dogs exhibiting behavioural changes such as visual impairment, urinary incontinence, arthritic pain or metabolic disorders such as thyroid or adrenal gland dysfunction need a full physical examination by a veterinary surgeon to determine whether these are simply the underlying health problems needing to be addressed or whether, in fact, they are suffering from canine cognitive dysfunction, as the symptom of disorientation is exhibited in several conditions and may be misleading.

Other Behavioural Changes Common in Older Dogs

Older dogs do seem to rest more frequently than younger animals and this should be respected. Old dogs should be provided with a comfortable bed in a secluded area to which they can escape if they so wish.

These dogs are not exercising much anymore and so they need less food. Many animals will self-regulate and eat less voluntarily; others continue to eat whatever they are given and become obese as a consequence.

If your older dog has a reduced appetite, it should have a complete health check by a veterinary surgeon. If all is well, allow it to eat whatever it feels it needs, provided it does not begin to lose weight. There are many commercial foods available now that cater especially for the nutritional needs of the aged dog.

A reluctance towards exercise may be due to arthritic change in the limbs or spine. Or it may be that your dog has a heart condition. If it has become slow and seems stiff, take it to your veterinary surgeon for a check up. There are some effective and safe drugs available to relieve arthritic pain. Owners are often so thrilled to see their old dog moving with renewed vigour once it is free of arthritic pain. The drugs work by reducing painful inflammation, and replacing the constituents of joint fluid.

Above *This old dog is losing control of his hindquarters as a result of degenerative changes. His gait is abnormal, hence his reluctance to walk anywhere.*

Behavioural changes consistent with old age
- Increased time sleeping or resting.
- Reduced food intake.
- Reduced exercise tolerance or willingness to exercise.
- Reduced tolerance towards children and other animals.
- Reduction in alertness, the dog is less easily roused.
- Bed-wetting.
- Shortness of breath.
- Raspy breathing, especially in Labradors or Labrador crosses.

Above *There are many causes of a decreased appetite in older dogs: bad teeth, a sore neck or one of a number of health problems such as gastrointestinal abnormalities and diabetes that are treatable, or at least manageable.*

Heart disease can be managed to improve your dog's quality of life. One of the most common age-related heart conditions is congestive heart failure. Affected dogs may puff and pant, and often cough during exercise as well as when they first get up after resting. In this condition, the valves between the heart chambers no longer function efficiently, so blood can leak back through them causing congestion and discomfort. As a result, the heart muscle has to work harder to move blood around the body and, with time, it becomes weakened.

Drugs are given to reduce lung congestion, which stops the coughing, dilates the blood vessels so that it is easier for blood to flow out of the heart and sometimes helps the heart muscle contract more strongly.

Reduced tolerance towards children and other animals can be the result of arthritic pain, or failing sight. If a dog is in pain, it may be afraid of being hurt by a child bumping into it. If it cannot hear well, being touched may startle it while sound asleep, and it could growl and snap out of self-defence before it realizes what is happening.

If your dog appears disoriented and canine cognitive dysfunction has been ruled out, your dog may be deaf or its vision impaired. If it is blind, furniture should be kept in the same place and a consistent routine followed. If it is deaf but not visually impaired, hand signals should be used to direct and it should be kept on a lead during roadside walks.

Similarly, night-time wandering, when not the result of canine cognitive dysfunction, may be due to discomfort caused by untreated arthritis, and house soiling may be due to loss of muscle tone or decreased neurological function of your dog's bladder or bowel.

Bed-wetting is common in old dogs and may be due to a hormonal deficiency or a problem with the nerves that control the bladder sphincter. If your dog leaves wet patches where it sleeps, consult your veterinary surgeon. These problems can be treated. Note: dogs with this condition may become anxious if owners react angrily.

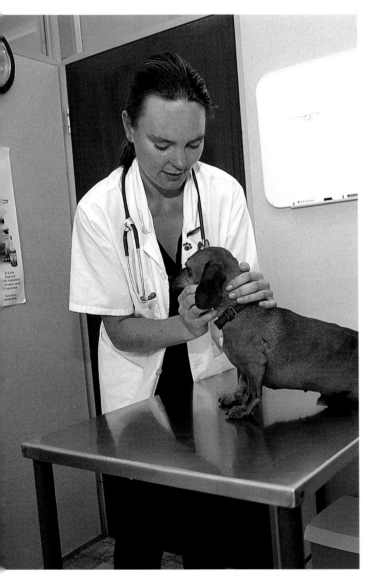

Above Cataracts are common in older dogs. The resulting visual impairment can cause dogs to move hesitantly, feel insecure and sometimes snap if approached suddenly. Cataracts can be surgically removed.

Left If your old dog seems to have developed noisy breathing, see your veterinary surgeon as treatment may be necessary. Ailing old dogs deserve your tender loving care. After their years of devotion, to you, they deserve it.

Shortness of breath and raspy breathing can be due to a condition known as laryngeal paralysis. In this condition, the nerve that controls the larynx starts to degenerate, so the dog cannot open it properly to take in air when it breathes. Dogs with this condition put a lot of energy into laboured breathing and therefore can't manage to do much in the way of exercise or play. Laryngeal paralysis can get to the point where the larynx will not open at all and the dog suffocates. This is treatable via surgery which ties the larynx open, allowing the dog to breathe properly.

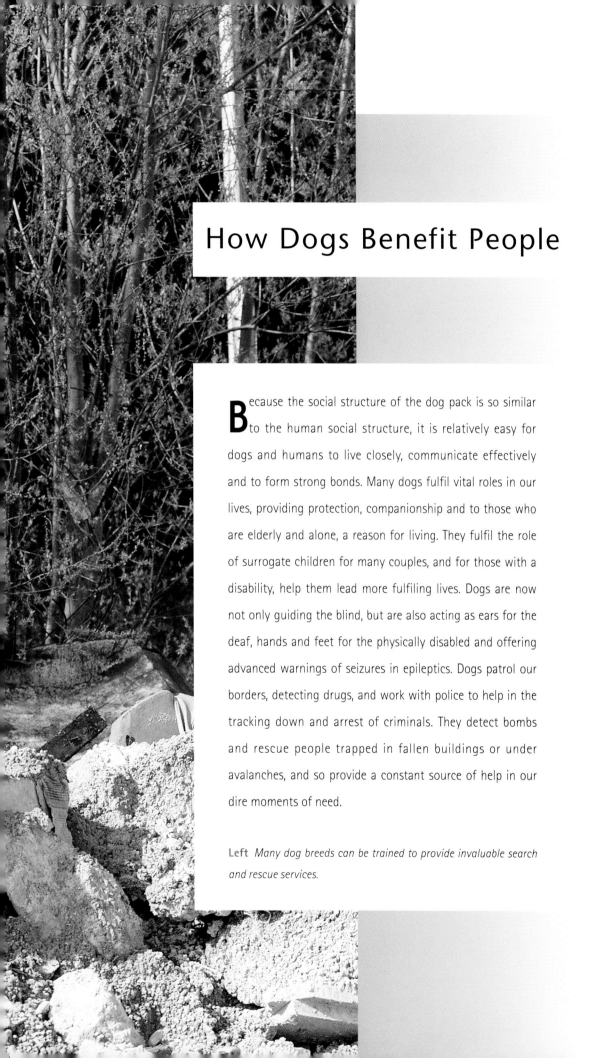

How Dogs Benefit People

Because the social structure of the dog pack is so similar to the human social structure, it is relatively easy for dogs and humans to live closely, communicate effectively and to form strong bonds. Many dogs fulfil vital roles in our lives, providing protection, companionship and to those who are elderly and alone, a reason for living. They fulfil the role of surrogate children for many couples, and for those with a disability, help them lead more fulfiling lives. Dogs are now not only guiding the blind, but are also acting as ears for the deaf, hands and feet for the physically disabled and offering advanced warnings of seizures in epileptics. Dogs patrol our borders, detecting drugs, and work with police to help in the tracking down and arrest of criminals. They detect bombs and rescue people trapped in fallen buildings or under avalanches, and so provide a constant source of help in our dire moments of need.

Left *Many dog breeds can be trained to provide invaluable search and rescue services.*

PET DOGS

In today's frenetic society some people find it difficult to form close communities. Families are fragmented and relatives often live far away from each other. In most suburbs it is rare for neighbours even to know each other's names. People can die in their homes without anyone noticing for days.

Like dogs, humans are social animals. They need companionship. A dog can make a good companion for a lonely person and vice versa. The dog greets its owner warmly, making him or her feel needed and appreciated. It is capable of surviving without humans if provided with some food source, however, in most cases pet dogs have no such opportunity and rely on the owner to open a can or packet, or cook something for them. This apparent dependence reinforces the bond.

For many elderly people, their dog is the centre of their world. It gives them a reason to get up in the morning, encourages them to take exercise, and provides them with love and companionship. Vera is an elderly client of mine whose life has been transformed by the arrival of Billy, a Jack Russell Terrier that she adopted from the pound.

Vera had been plagued by illness and had to have her 17-year-old blind dog put to sleep before going into hospital for major surgery. When she came home from hospital, she had an empty house. Recovering from her illness, Vera suffered from significant depression. She could hardly bring herself to get out of bed in the morning. She knew she had to do something and rang the pound. One of the dog-control officers brought Billy to meet her and left him with her for a week to see how they got on. Billy was a bright, active little dog with a great sense of fun. Vera liked him immediately and a bond quickly developed. Billy needed exercise so Vera was motivated to walk him along the waterfront twice daily.

This was just what she needed to improve her health. Billy slept on her bed and made sure that she got up to experience the beauty of the early morning. He curled up beside her at night on the sofa, resting his head on her knee while she watched her

Above *Elderly people can benefit greatly from the company of a dog. The dog provides a reason for them to get up in the morning, as well as companionship and comfort.*

favourite programmes on television. On two occasions, Billy has alerted Vera to pots boiling over on the stove, or burning dry. He runs and barks at her, then runs into the kitchen and barks again, continuing this behaviour until she follows him.

Billy loves riding in the car and motivates Vera to drive to the beach or to one of the parks. In this way, the little dog has helped Vera regain her physical and mental health.

It is nonsense to say that a person is too old to own a dog because they might die leaving it homeless. The sensible thing to do is to make provision for its ongoing care should this be necessary. In fact, no matter what age an owner is, thought should always be given to a dog's ongoing care in case of the owner's death by accident or illness.

Increasingly, young couples delay having a family or elect not to have children at all. For them a dog is often a child substitute, something that they can care for and nurture together. It can be taken on walks, outings to the beach or the park, or even to the café. It needs to be bathed and fed and can be bought toys and collars.

When a pet is lost through death by illness or accident, people go through a grieving process equivalent to that experienced by the loss of a human family member. Pets also grieve when they lose an owner or a companion pet. They often become very depressed, go off their food, and spend time sitting in areas that the pet or person frequented. They need a lot of love and attention and distractions to help them through their suffering.

In a strange way, seeing the pet grieve can help a bereaved partner get over her loss more rapidly. She wants to make the pet feel happier and thus makes the effort to do things for it, thereby taking her mind off her own grief.

GUIDE DOGS

Guide dogs make a wonderful difference to the lives of blind people. They learn to take their owners safely across roads, down stairs, onto transportation and to specific destinations such as shops or the doctor's surgery, the dogs remember the routes associated with the destinations.

Guide dogs undergo very strict selection criteria and are intensively trained. It is a hard job for them to do as they must be constantly aware of their owner's needs and safety.

Below *It is nonsense to say that a person is too old to own a dog. The animal here is still getting adequate care and exercise from his elderly owner. Provision can be made for ongoing care of the dog should its owner pass on.*

They must not be distracted by sensory stimuli in their surroundings. Many fail the training course because they just cannot resist food on the street or because they are too protective of their handlers. They have to learn to modify their natural behaviour to suit their owner's needs. Those that pass the course do their jobs extremely well.

When they are in harness, they are in work mode; when they are free of the harness they can behave naturally.

DEAF-ASSIST DOGS

These dogs are trained to alert their owners to everyday noises such as the doorbell, the telephone, the smoke alarm or something burning on the stove. These dogs are usually of a mixed breed and are often also rescue dogs.

Above *A guide dog is the greatest gift that a blind person can receive as it is skilled at taking its owners safely across roads, down stairs, onto transportation and to specific destinations such as shops or the doctor's surgery.*

Much of what they do builds on natural behaviour. Most dogs will bark when someone rings the doorbell, many of them will bark in response to the telephone and will become concerned at unusual sounds on the stove. These behaviours are encouraged and reinforced so that the dog learns to paw at and generally bother the owner to alert her to important sounds, and not give up until the owner has taken some action.

DISABILITY DOGS

Dogs are used increasingly to assist people with limited mobility. They are trained to open doors, fetch clothing, fetch telephones, fetch walking sticks, fetch the mail and even to load and unload washing machines and dryers.

Due to this assistance, these dogs make a huge difference to their owner's lives, helping them to be partly independent of other humans: for some disabled people, the constant presence of a human helper is bad for their self-esteem, making them feel inadequate.

Below *A disability dog provides service and comfort to its housebound owner, particularly as the animal removes the owner's dependence on other human beings.*

The dog is both companion and helper and does not watch its owner with pity or condescension. In fact, the dogs seem to really enjoy their daily tasks and will often spontaneously bring objects to their owners which they think they might require.

EPILEPSY-ALERT DOGS

It has recently been documented that some dogs seem to sense when their epileptic owners are going to have a seizure. It is as yet unclear just how they know this. It may be that the person's scent changes, or they may be picking up changes in electrical activity in their owner's brain. It may even be as simple as subtle changes in body language.

As yet there are no scientific studies confirming that dogs will alert consistently to every seizure, although there are owners who swear they do. Many owners describe how their dog often stares and paws at them, whines and generally behaves out of character.

Owners soon learn that if their dog behaves in this way, they are about to seizure and can then seek help, or sit or lie down so that they do not get hurt by falling with the onset of the fit.

The dogs, otherwise known as epilepsy-alert dogs, have an innate ability which is enhanced by training. The dog's natural behaviour is reinforced and it is disciplined to do things such as fetch a pouch of medication or seek help. The dog also has to learn to trust other people to approach and assist its owner.

Epilepsy-alert dogs need to be strongly bonded to their owners. A dog that is kept outside and only has limited contact with its owner is unlikely to alert during the onset of a seizure or help its owner feel secure.

The training procedure for these dogs involves teaching them how to behave in public areas, namely, how to be calm and focused on their owner in a crowded restaurant or on public transport. It also teaches them to accept that other people carrying medical equipment may need to approach their extremely vulnerable owner in a rushed and threatening manner.

The alerting behaviour of the dogs is reinforced, and they have a daily practice routine that may involve fetching objects or finding a particular person who may assist their owner, such as a family member. Having a dog opens up a new world to people suffering from epilepsy.

When Jackie, an attractive, vivacious 18-year-old studying to become a social worker, was diagnosed with epilepsy, her world collapsed. She was having four seizures daily, and couldn't drive, work or study. Her medication made her tired and depressed. She became afraid to venture outside.

Jackie's father bought her a puppy as a companion. The Golden Retriever cross whom she named Zac was cute and fluffy and very bright. He became the centre of her world. When Zac was about six months old, he began to behave in a difficult manner. He frequently jumped and pawed at Jackie, refusing to sit down, and at times knocking her over. The family was disappointed. Zac had been to training school and had done really well. Why was he behaving so badly now? They decided if it didn't stop they would have to find him a new home.

Jackie took Zac to an animal psychologist, who made the connection that there was a pattern to his behaviour. Zac would begin behaving strangely 10 to 20 minutes before Jackie had a seizure. At all other times he would behave normally. Thus, each time he was alerting Jackie to an oncoming seizure.

They went to a special training school where Zac was taught to alert Jackie in a more controlled manner and Jackie learned to listen to him. He was also taught to fetch her medication and to alert family members.

Jackie found that with many of her seizures, if she sat down and relaxed at the onset, they would be very mild, and pass quickly. Zac would alert her in time for her to achieve this. Having Zac changed Jackie's life; she had the confidence to leave home and even finished her degree.

Left *Border-patrol dogs are vital in the detection of illicit drugs and foodstuffs.*

BORDER-PATROL DOGS

These dogs are taught to detect the presence of drugs and foodstuffs on travellers and in their luggage. At first, the dogs are taught scent discrimination as a game, and then taught to apply this to work situations.

They learn to detect and then alert by sitting in front of the object or person carrying the forbidden goods. They are rewarded with a game and a lot of attention. Border-patrol dogs need to have a high play drive to be suitable for this type of work. They also need to be able to remain focused and be comfortable in crowded, noisy situations. These dogs are highly useful in keeping drug trafficking under control.

DETECTING DISEASE

There are reports that dogs can detect cancer. As yet there is insufficient scientific data to verify this absolutely, but there are some interesting reports on the topic.

One of the earliest reports was published in the 1989 edition of *The Lancet*, an international journal of medical science and practice. A Border Collie cross belonging to a British woman repeatedly sniffed a mole on her owner's leg. She even tried to bite it off. The woman eventually decided to have the mole checked and it was diagnosed as a malignant melanoma!

In another report a Labrador took excessive interest in a lesion on its owner's leg; it turned out to be a basal cell carcinoma.

A dermatologist, Armand Cognetta, was fascinated by this and worked with a police dog handler to train dogs to locate tissue samples containing melanomas. They achieved close to a 100 per cent detection rate. Other researchers are exploring the possibility of training dogs to detect prostate cancer by sniffing urine samples.

Above *Police dogs are wonderful assistants for their handlers, helping in the tracking down and disarming of criminals.*

POLICE DOGS

Police dogs are important members of the force. Their acute sense of smell is used to detect human scent and to follow a trail for long distances. The police force benefits from their natural predatory aggression and instinct to guard and protect by training them to apprehend suspects once they have been tracked down. They are taught how to avoid injury by taking hold of the weapon-bearing arm of a suspect. Many police officers have a police dog to thank for saving them from injury or death.

RESCUE DOGS

Dogs are used for search and rescue in natural disasters such as earthquakes and avalanches where people may be trapped beneath snow or rubble and are undetectable to rescuers on the surface.

Having an acute sense of hearing and smell, dogs can detect trapped people and will alert searchers to their presence. These dogs also need a high play drive to remain motivated to perform this work. They are taught scent discrimination and they learn how to fetch and locate a handler buried in snow or under debris. When they locate the person, they receive an ecstatic greeting from their owner and lots of praise.

These dogs have to learn to ride on snowmobiles and need to become familiarized with being dropped down or winched up by helicopters. It is a lot to ask of them, but they do it well and willingly.

Below *People buried in avalanches owe their discovery and survival to the wonderful dogs trained to search and find them.*

FARM DOGS

Working dogs on farms are important extensions of their owners. Sheep dogs are invaluable in finding individual sheep, bringing them together and driving flocks.

During the training process their natural instincts to round up and drive prey animals are exploited but. they are selectively bred and trained so that the predatory aspect of this behaviour is not carried through to an overt attack.

Dogs can move large numbers of sheep over long distances and rough terrain. The task would take people far longer and could even prove impossible. These dogs, however, have an amazing ability to weigh up a situation and to predict an outcome.

Above *A trusted working member on the farm, this Border Collie is accustomed to interacting with animals; rounding flocks of geese, guarding livestock and herding sheep.*

While working on a sheep farm as a student I was sent to bring a flock of sheep down to the yards with a young dog which was in training. The sheep were difficult to move and kept breaking away and running back up the hill. Jack, an experienced dog belonging to the farmer, suddenly ran towards me, rounded up the mob and took them through to the yards. There was no one else around. He had summed up the situation and acted to remedy the problem.

Dogs and other Pets

Dogs can co-exist successfully with many other animals and, in fact, often form close associations with them. This probably happens more commonly when puppies are introduced to other species at a young age, although sometimes bonds can develop quite unexpectedly between adult dogs and animals of other species. As with all aspects of behaviour, the way dogs relate to other animals is influenced by their genetic make-up, their environment, their state of health and past experiences. If you own stock or small furry animals, and are planning on getting a dog, choose a breed that does not have a high predatory drive and if possible, opt for a puppy. If you do get an older dog, seek advice from an animal behaviourist on how to integrate it into your home.

Left *Dogs and cats can learn to have mutual respect for each other if they are introduced to each other at a young age.*

When selecting a pet dog to fit in with the family cat, the guinea pigs and pet rabbits, it is sensible to select a breed that is not highly predatory. It would be easier to integrate a Bichon Frise than a Jack Russell, more so than a Greyhound, into such a situation.

If you ride horses and want a dog that will adapt well to them and accompany you out on rides, a Dalmatian may be the right dog for you. These dogs were bred to accompany horse-drawn carriages and to guard them at night. As a breed the Dalmatian has a special empathy for horses and it has the stamina to accompany a rider over long distances.

Of course there are always exceptions, and I am describing trends, not absolutes. There are individual Greyhounds that snuggle up with cats, and terriers that play gently with pet rabbits. It is, however, useful to know what to expect from a breed as a general rule. Guard dogs do not generally have a problem integrating with other animals, as is the case with lap dogs. Dogs that may cause difficulties with other pets include gun dogs, hunting dogs such as terriers and sight hounds, and some herding dogs.

Above Gun dogs, such as this Springer Spaniel, are known for fetching dead or injured birds and will return them to their owner without damaging them in any way.

INTERSPECIES COMPATIBILITY

As discussed, dogs have been selectively bred over many years to behave in certain ways. Some breeds such as terriers and sight hounds have been selected for hunting skills and so have a strong predatory drive. Others such as collies have been selected to be less predatory to assist with the care and management of stock, while King Charles Cavalier Spaniels, Toy Poodles and Bichon Frises have been bred primarily as companions, usually showing little or no predatory behaviour. Selection for territorial aggression in guard dogs, such as Rottweilers and Doberman Pinschers, has little bearing on their relationships with other animals.

Gun dogs

Gun dogs such as Springer Spaniels, German Short-haired Pointers and Weimaraners are bred to assist with hunting in one form or another and thus have a high retrieval instinct and soft mouths.

These dogs are happy to fetch a dead or injured bird and will return it to their owner without attempting to eat it, and usually without damaging it in any way. They show a strong tendency to chase, track and flush birds, even if they are never taken into a hunting situation. They can be taught to leave domestic hens or ducks alone, but it is very difficult to stop them chasing a bird that is flushed from the bush or a field during a walk.

They also have a high exercise requirement and tend to be excitable, so if you live on a small section of land with a few chickens and occasionally enjoy a quiet stroll through the park to feed the ducks, it may not be wise to choose a gun dog breed.

Herding dogs

This type of dog has been selectively bred to form a close association with stock and to protect them from predators. Maremma Shepherds, in particular, are left alone in the hills with flocks of sheep. Their pale coats blend with the colour of the sheep and they are happy to spend hours wandering with the flock, defending it against all kinds of predators such as wolves.

Border Collies, on the other hand, are selected for their strong herding instinct, an attribute that is derived from predatory behaviour but falls short of the attack-and-kill sequence. These dogs have such a strong urge to round up stock that they will try and herd domestic hens, and have even been known to round up fish in large indoor aquaria!

It is rare for herding dogs to harm stock or pet animals. Sometimes, however, if they have not been well trained or if a dog from the city suddenly comes face to face with sheep or other stock, the innate chase instinct may well be taken one step further, leading to injury.

Hunting dogs

Terriers including the Jack Russell, Fox, Lakeland and Border Terrier, and sight hounds such as Greyhounds and Deerhounds are bred to be highly predatory and may represent a significant risk to other pets, digging out and killing small furry creatures. This usually includes cats, especially if they have hunting experience, although terriers that have grown up with cats may learn to accept and even bond with them.

Greyhounds, especially those that have raced, really need to be kept away from pet cats. Their chase instinct is very strong and if they see a cat run off in front of them, they will tend to run it down. If they catch it, they are likely to kill it.

Below *Border Collies have a strong herding instinct and willingly spend hours herding sheep. They are also well known among stock-dog enthusiasts for gathering, sorting and moving ranch cattle.*

INTRODUCING A NEW PET

Dogs that are exposed to other animals in a positive manner from puppyhood, and regularly throughout their lives, respond well to new pets compared with dogs that have never been exposed to other animals or that have been encouraged to treat other animals as prey.

Cats

Dogs that grow up with a cat or kitten from a young age will play with and often sleep snuggled up to it. Because they are familiar with cats, they may even mother orphaned kittens. Male dogs as well as females may exhibit this behaviour. Surprisingly, the small helpless creatures do not evoke predatory aggression in these animals rather, they seem to arouse maternal and paternal instincts.

If a puppy has been introduced to an adult cat that is not especially fond of dogs, it may receive one or two well-placed swats on the nose, and may develop a healthy respect for that cat and learn to avoid it. In such situations, although household cats may have become accepted as part of the 'pack', most dogs may still chase other cats.

Some dogs of breeds that have not been selected for predatory drive may be on friendly terms with any cat that stands its ground but may give chase if it runs, a response triggered by the movement which is part of the predatory sequence of behaviour: stalking, chasing, capturing and killing. These dogs, however, do not complete the sequence – they do not kill the cat if they catch up to it. On the other hand, breeds that have been selected for predatory drive, such as terriers, are likely to attack a cat on sight whether or not it is moving. They complete the predatory sequence and this frequently ends in the cat's death.

Sheep

Pet dogs brought up on sheep farms may cease to consider lambs as prey animals. Dogs of either sex may mother orphan lambs that are being hand-reared, licking them and showing concern when they bleat. As they grow, they may regard them as playmates and spend time playing chasing games with them, much as they would with a puppy.

Adult dogs that have never been exposed to lambs are likely to harm them. This can be a problem where farms border suburban areas and pet dogs are not controlled. Pet dogs left to roam free will form packs and may attack, severely wound and sometimes kill large numbers of sheep.

Below Surprisingly, these kittens do not evoke predatory aggression in this male dog. Rather, they seem to arouse paternal instincts in him.

Above *When taking your dog for a run on the beach be aware of horses in the area and remember to steer well clear of them.*

Horses

Some dogs develop very strong bonds with horses and may play with and sleep close to them. Many dogs can learn to accompany their owners on horse treks. They learn how to stay at a safe distance to avoid being accidentally trampled or kicked. Some can be taught to lead horses by taking the halter rope in their teeth.

Dogs that have had no experience with horses may instinctively avoid danger. Nevertheless, it is wise not to assume this and to keep inexperienced dogs out of fields where horses are grazing.

Small furry animals

Rabbits are irresistible targets for many dogs. They are small, fluffy, move erratically and taste good! Despite this it is possible for dogs and rabbits to live happily together.

Several years ago I had a dog that grew up with my pet rabbits. She used to watch over them as they took their exercise outside. If I wanted to bring them in, and one refused to come, she would run up to it and lie beside it with her chin firmly placed on its back, holding it there until I arrived to pick it up. She never chased or barked at them. On the other hand, wild rabbits were fair game.

IMPORTANT GUIDELINES

The most important points to remember when introducing dogs and puppies to other household pets are:

- Do not expect a dog to view another pet as you do.
- Take it slowly.
- Be very clear about your expectations.
- Try to make all interactions positive for both animals.
- Be aware that the dynamics of the relationships between the dog and other pets may change when you are not present, so minimize potential risks.

Adult dogs and kittens

If you bring a new kitten home, it is important to introduce it to an adult dog carefully. Keep the kitten in a separate room for the first two or three days and allow the dog to become accustomed to the smell and sound of it without actually seeing it.

The dog will probably spend time listening and sniffing at the door. Eventually it will probably lose interest and accept that something is in there to stay. At this point you can progress to bringing the kitten out into the same room as the dog. The dog should be on a lead and the kitten should either be closely supervised by another person or in a cage.

At the first few meetings, the dog should be asked to sit quietly and watch the kitten at a distance. If the dog is particularly excitable, it is much easier and safer to have the kitten in a cage during these sessions. Once the dog is sitting quietly and is listening to you, remove the kitten from the room. Reward quiet behaviour. Continue doing this until the dog becomes accustomed to the kitten's presence in the room and shows less interest in it.

Now allow the dog to sniff at the kitten in the cage; if it barks or growls at the kitten or becomes overexcited, remove the dog from the room. When the dog is calmer with the kitten and can approach it in a friendly manner, allow them to come into contact. Have the kitten running free and the dog on a lead. If the dog growls at or attempts to attack the kitten, squirt it with a water pistol, ask it to sit and then reward it for calm, quiet behaviour. When they are able to interact calmly or playfully, allow them to mix freely.

Puppies and adult cats

When a puppy is first brought home, the resident cat is likely to react in one of three ways. It may take one look and run for cover, coming back gradually to investigate in its own time. It may approach boldly to investigate the newcomer and assert itself immediately with a well-placed swipe of the paw if the puppy is too bold; or it may show no interest at all in the puppy, avoiding it at all costs.

When the puppy arrives, it will spend a great deal of time in a relatively confined area. This is usually soon recognized by the cat who will probably make a point of frequenting the areas that it knows the puppy cannot access. If the puppy is kept behind a gate, then puppy and cat can gradually become accustomed to each other. As the puppy grows and is allowed more freedom, so they will be able to interact more freely.

One of the first things to do when bringing a puppy into a household with an adult cat is to have the cat's claws clipped. Ask your veterinary surgeon to do this. If you feel confident, you could buy some nail clippers and trim them yourself every six to eight weeks.

This procedure is not painful but some cats object to having it done and it can be difficult to hold the cat and clip the claws yourself. The reason for doing this is to avoid the possibility of the puppy being clawed in the eye. This is a common injury when puppies are introduced to cats and can result in the puppy losing an eye.

Encourage the puppy to be quiet around the cat and not to bark at it. Spend some time cuddling the cat close to the puppy. Make sure the cat receives some special attention at a specific time every day so that it does not feel left out. Usually relations between puppy and cat are sorted within two months of their introduction to each other. They either become firm friends or develop mutual tolerance.

Rabbits, guinea pigs and birds

Adult dogs can learn to accept rabbits, guinea pigs and birds, and to do them no harm. Start by involving the dog (on a lead) with the daily care of your smaller pets. Allow the dog to sniff at the cage and to watch you clean it and feed the animals or birds.

Left *With patience and care on behalf of its owner, a dog can learn to live in harmony with pet birds, even though it is a predatory animal. The first interaction between dogs and birds should always be supervised.*

Ask the dog to sit quietly beside you and watch the animals at play. Have a water pistol handy and if the dog attempts to lunge at the animals, say 'no' and squirt it. Then ask it to sit and reward it.

Once the dog has accepted the creatures, start allowing them to run freely. Keep the dog on a lead and ask it to sit and relax. Allow it to sniff at the animals gently if they approach. If the dog snaps, use the water pistol again.

Continue in this way until the dog remains quiet and relaxed yet interested in the small animals, or totally ignores them, showing no interest at all. Then you can attempt to allow the dog free interaction with the other pets. Supervise this for one or two weeks, then, depending on the dog, you may be able to leave them free together, unsupervised.

If you decide to do this, have a dog-proof safe haven into which the animals can run should they feel threatened. There are some dogs that will be very accepting of small fluffy pets when owners are present but are likely to attack them when the owners are away.

Bear this in mind, and check the animals after 10 minutes when you do leave them alone together, unsupervised. It is probably unwise to leave the dog and small pets interacting freely together when you are away from the property. Even rough play by the dog may result in injury to a rabbit or guinea pig. A squeal of objection to a roughly placed paw may trigger a predatory response and result in tragedy.

As regards puppies, when they are brought up with other household pets they are usually very accepting of them and not interested in chasing or harming them. There are exceptions, however, and it is wise not to leave a puppy and small pets unsupervised. Allow the puppy to be involved with the care of the small pets and reprimand rough play. Ensure that a territorial rabbit or hen does not hurt it; try to make all its experiences with these animals positive ones.

Above *Some dogs develop very strong bonds with horses and are often found playing around them.*

Horses

When first introducing puppies or adult dogs to horses, do so from the other side of a fence. Allow the horse to sniff the puppy and vice versa. If there is any aggression shown by the dog, remove it from the situation.

Progress to having the puppy tied or put in a crate or pen nearby while you groom and ride the horse. Do this until horse and puppy are quite relaxed in the situation. Now allow the puppy to roam freely but under supervision. Ask it to sit and stay in the area where it is usually tied up. Teach it a 'keep out' command by squirting it with a water pistol if it comes too close for safety.

Most dogs seem to have an innate understanding of the dangers involved in approaching a horse's heels, but others are less cautious. It is important to teach them because a well-placed kick from an iron-clad hoof can seriously injure or even kill your dogs.

Glossary

Alpha roll: A highly controversial method of disciplining dogs which involves forcibly rolling the dog onto its back and holding it until it stops struggling. Some trainers advocate it as a means to assert dominance over a dog.

Arthritis: A progressive disease in mammals characterized by the slow disintegration of the cartilage in the joints followed by the degradation of surrounding bone.

Bandage protector spray: A spray with an unpleasant smell and taste that is used to prevent dogs from biting at and removing bandages.

Barometric pressure: Atmospheric pressure as indicated by a barometer.

Behavioural medicine: The use of medication to treat behavioural problems.

Behavioural science: The scientific study of animal behaviour, including dog behaviour.

Behavioural zoology: As above.

Binocular vision: The ability to see with both eyes; with dogs, in particular, their peripheral vision is much wider than ours, about 70 degrees more, which gives them a greater awareness of movement.

Boarding kennels: A substitute home for many dogs whose owners are temporarily unable to take care of them.

Breed standard: A written description of what the ideal specimen of a given breed should look like.

Cross-breed: A type of dog produced by the mating of two different breeds.

Deference: A dog's act of submission in its interaction with other dogs or obedient yielding in response to the wishes of its owner, in order to confirm its standing in the social hierarchy of its human and canine 'pack'.

Desensitization protocol: A process of neutralizing a dog's abnormal fear responses to certain stimuli which is conducted by a qualified animal behaviourist or a veterinary animal behaviourist, depending on the type and severity of the problem, in a controlled environment.

Dogsitters: Professionals who look after your dogs on a daily basis at your home during the time you are at work.

Enzymatic cleaner: Any cleaning preparation that contains enzymes as an active ingredient. These remove all residual substances and, therefore, odours.

Euthanasia: The act of humanely ending, by lethal injection, the life of an animal suffering from a terminal disease or an incurable condition.

Fear memory: A dog's abnormal response of fear to a particular stimulus caused by a negative introduction to that stimulus at an early developmental phase as a puppy. This can occur in its fear-imprint period of between eight and 10 weeks, and 16 weeks of age, and memory of this incident can be triggered by sight, sound or smell cues. A fear memory can also be produced in animals of any age as the result of a traumatic experience.

Fly ball: A ball game of 'catch' that owners play with their dog based on the development of retrieval skills with the exception that the ball is thrown vertically within a metre of the owner and the dog catches it mid-air. It can also be played by using a machine that is operated by a foot pedal releasing a spring that launches the ball into the air. Dogs can be taught to load the machine by themselves and press the foot pedal allowing them to play retrieve happily all day without involving people.

Foghorn: A modified loud-horn or hooter.

GABA: Accronym for gamma-aminobutyric acid, a biologically active substance found in brain.

Give eye: A form of predatory stalk often seen in Border Collies used as herding dogs. When controlling sheep, they approach head-on and stare intently at the sheep, intimidating them into moving away. This is often referred to as 'giving eye'.

Halti: A head-collar used as a restraint while walking or training dogs.

In-breeding: Mating of closely related dogs.

Larynx: The part of the respiratory tract between the pharynx and the trachea, having walls of cartilage and muscle and containing the vocal cords enveloped in folds of mucous.

Line breeding: Mating of related dogs within a family or related to a common ancestor.

Mounting: A male dog's act of climbing onto a female dog for copulation, also sometimes re-enacted by female and male adolescent dogs on people's legs and pieces of furniture as a sign of dominance, and often seen among small puppies during play.

Medial canthus: An anatomical term used to describe the inner corner of a dog's eye behind which lies a tear duct.

Neuron: The impulse-conducting cells in mammals that make up the brain, spinal cord and nerves.

Neuter: The act of castration.

Nictitating membrane: A 'third eyelid' which comes across the dog's eye when the animal is asleep and helps to keep the eye moist and protected.

Olfactory cells: The countless cells located in a dog's nose which enable it to acutely pick up scent, especially that of other dogs via glands found on either side of the head, neck and perineal area which secrete a substance enabling it to know their social and reproductive status.

Perineal area: The region between the scrotum and the anus in male dogs, and between the vaginal junction and the anus in bitches.

Posture: A term used to describe the head, ear and tail position as well as hair pattern of a dog, attributes which indicate its mood and intention.

Predatory drive: A dog's innate impulse to stalk and catch prey, with attributes characteristic of its breeding.

Predatory aggression: Aggression shown during the act of catching and killing prey. This response is triggered in dogs by the sight of prey or prey equivalent as well as by the erratic movements of small children.

Puppy preschool: Group training and socialization classes for young puppies. Often run by veterinary clinics.

Reactive breeds: Breeds with high activity levels that are quick to react to stimuli.

Serotonin: A chemical, secreted by the thalamus in the brains of mammals, which is responsible for feelings of contentedness and calm. It is an organic compound, $C10H12N2O$, formed from an essential amino acid called tryptophan.

Service dogs: Also known as mobility dogs. Service dogs are trained to assist physically disabled people, to accomplish everyday activities that they would not normally be able to accomplish on their own. They are also trained in a number of safety procedures.

Shadow chasing: An obsessive-compulsive disorder in which a dog will chase shadows without end.

Signalling: A method of communication or signalling among dogs that maintains their social hierarchy without constant fighting. A lower-ranking animal's signals to a dog with a higher standing include a lowered head, averted gaze, tail pointing down and wagging, and ears back. It may roll on its side exposing its throat and stomach, signalling complete submission. The higher-ranking animal maintains an upright posture with straight tail and direct gaze.

Sire and dam: The male and female parent of a domesticated animal, in particular that of the dog.

Tail biting: An obsessive-compulsive disorder in which a dog will run around in circles biting its tail for excessively long periods of time.

Territorial: A dog's innate drive to protect its territory and that of its owner.

The 'aunty' system: A daily system whereby friends and family look after your dog when you are at work.

Thyroid: A gland found in mammals responsible for the secretion of thyroxin which controls the metabolic processes in the body.

Toy breeds: Incredibly small breeds or very small versions of a particular breed such as in the case of a Toy Poodle which is the tiniest poodle you can get.

Vaccinations: An inoculation administered to dogs to prevent the development of particular diseases.

Veterinary clinic: Clinic at which veterinary surgeons treat sick or injured animals and perform routine surgery.

Vocalize: Make a noise using the vocal chords such as in the case of barking, howling and whining.

Yard: An enclosed tract of land in which animals such as chickens and pigs, and in this case dogs, are kept.

Index

Contacts & Further Reading

ASSOCIATIONS

America
• ANIMAL BEHAVIOR SOCIETY
Dr Janis Driscoll, Dept. of Physiology,
Campus PO Box 173364,
Denver, CO 80217-3364.

• AMERICAN COLLEGE OF VETERINARY
BEHAVIORISTS,
Dr Katherine Houpt, Secretary,
Dept. of Physiology, College of Veterinary
Medicine, Cornell University, Ithica,
NY 14853-6401.

• AMERICAN PET ASSOCIATION
PO Box 7172 Boulder, CO 80306-7172.
Tel: Main 800-APA-PETS (800-272-7387);
E-mail: apa@apapets.org
www.apapets.com

• AMERICAN VETERINARY SOCIETY OF ANIMAL
BEHAVIOR
Dr Debra Horwitz, Secretary/Treasurer,
Veterinary Behavior Consultations,
253 S. Graeser Road, St Louis, MO 63141.

• ASSOCIATION OF PET DOG TRAINERS
PO Box 3734, Salinas, CA 93912-3734.
Tel: (408) 663 9257; 1(800)PET-DOGS;
www.apdt.com

• CANINE UNIVERSITY
71 Clinton Street, Malden, MA 02148,
Tel: (781) 324 3722;
E-mail: training@canineuniversity.com
www.canineuniversity.com

• NATIONAL ASSOCIATION OF DOG
OBEDIENCE INSTRUCTORS
(Kim Blyler, NADOI #358), Secretary,
PMB #369 729 , Grapevine Highway,
Hurst, TX 76054-2085.
E-mail: email@nadoi.org
www.nadoi.org

• PROFESSIONAL ANIMAL BEHAVIOR ASSOCIATES
PO Box 25111, London, Ontario N6C 6A8.
Tel: (519) 685 4756;
Fax: (519) 685 6618

• THE ASSOCIATION FOR BEHAVIOR ANALYSIS
(Anna Blackwell), 3303 59th Ave, South
West Seattle, WA 98116.

UK
• BRITISH VETERINARY ASSOCIATION
7 Mansfield Street, London, W1G 9NQ
Tel: (020) 7636 6541;
Fax: (020) 7436 2970;
E-mail: bvahq@bva.co.uk

• FEDERATION OF DOG TRAINERS AND CANINE
BEHAVIOURISTS
15 Lightburne Ave,
Lytham St Annes, Lancs, FY8 1JE.
E-mail: gen@fdtcb.com
www.fdtcb.com

• THE ASSOCIATION OF PET BEHAVIOUR
COUNSELLORS
PO BOX 46, Worcester, WR8 9YS.
Tel: (0) 1386 751151;
Fax: (0) 1386 750743;
E-mail: apbc@petbcent.demon.co.uk
www.apbc.org.uk

• THE BLUE CROSS
Shilton Road, Burford, Oxon OX18 4PF,
Tel: (0) 1993 825500;
Fax: (0) 1993 823083;
www.thebluecross.org.uk

BOOKS
• DOG: A PRACTICAL GUIDE TO CARING FOR YOUR
DOG, Dr David Sands, Collins

• DOG LANGUAGE
Roger Abrantes, Wakan Tanka Publishers

• THE EVERYTHING DOG TRAINING AND TRICKS
BOOK
Gerilyn J. Bielakiewicz, Adam Media
Corporation

• WHAT IS MY DOG THINKING?
.Gwen Bailey, Hamlyn

PERIODICALS
• DOGS MONTHLY
RTC Associates, High Street, Ascot,
Berkshire, SL57JG

• DOG SPORTS MAGAZINE
DSM Publishing Inc., 940 Tyger Street,
Studio 17, Benicia, CA 94510-2916

• DOG TRAINING WEEKLY
4/5 Feidr Castell, Business Park, Fishguard,
Pembrokeshire, SA 659BB

• DOG WORLD
29 N, Wada Drive, Chicago, IL 60606

• OFF LEAD (Training magazine)
PO Drawer A, Clark Mills, NY 13321

• WHOLE DOG
1175 Regent Street, Alameda, CA 94501,
Email: WholeDogJ@aol.com
www.whole-dog-journal.com

WEBSITES
Australia
• PAWS 4 FUN: Behaviour and Training
www4.tpgi.com.au

• PETS PLAYGROUND: New Directions for
Australian Pet Owners
www.petsplayground.com.au/

International
• INTERNATIONAL ASSOCIATION OF CANINE
PROFESSIONALS
PO Box 560156, Montverde,
FL 34756-0156, USA
Tel: (407) 469-2008;
E-mail: iacp@mindspring.com
www.dogpro.org

• WORLD ANIMAL NET
Eastern Hemisphere,
24 Barleyfields, Didcot,
Oxon OX11 0BJ, United Kingdom,
Tel/Fax: (1235) 210 775
E-mail: info@worldanimal.net

Western Hemisphere,
19 Chestnut Square, Boston,
MA 02130, USA
Tel: (617) 524 3670;
Fax: (617) 524 1815;
www.worldanimalnet.org

New Zealand
DOLITTLE TRAINING
www.dolittle-training.com

Acknowledgements

New Holland Publishers would like to thank the following people, on behalf of principal photographer,
Dorothée von der Osten, for their cooperation and assistance on photoshoots: Dr Stevens: *Penzance Veterinary Clinic,* Hout Bay;
Neels Trosky & 'Wonder': *The SA Guide Dogs Association for the Blind*; Karl Brüseke; Glenn Collins; Lauren and Daniela Fonto;
Rohan Ridley; Carin Martens; Marizelle Strydom & 'Rex', Annemarie Baalbergen, Beryl Erikson & 'Oliver'; Mrs Clough & 'Dipstick';
Dr M. T. de Villiers: *Kloof Veterinary Hospital*; Elizabeth, Stefan, Matteo and Carlo Milandri; Ann and Mike Gillard & 'Eddy';
Brenda and Arjan Buikema & 'Zeika', 'Jackson' and 'Metisse'; Mr and Mrs A. Kalis; Rachel Finlayson; Lesley Manning; Rosy Finlayson;
Karen Gray-Kilfoil; Ursula and Bert von Sethe & 'Nelson'; Hylke and Dean Preston; Mark Brown & 'Jack'; Tracy du Plessis and
Shane Smart & 'Zack'; Jerri Mperdempes & 'Rudi'; Leigh and Trent Brown & 'Goose'; Kirsten Howard and the Broughten family.

PHOTOGRAPHIC CREDITS

All photography by Dorothée von der Osten for New Holland Image Library (NHIL), with the exception of the following
photographers and/or their agencies. Copyright rests with these individuals and/or their agencies:

Page	Loc	Credit	Page	Loc	Credit	Page	Loc	Credit	Page	Loc	Credit
Front cover		WP/JB	42		GM	54	tl	JT	83		SL
1		DO	43		DO	54	br	GM	84		DO
6–7		DO	44	br	GM	55	tl/br	GM	86–87		WP/JB
15	tr	IF	45	br	AL/JDM	59		SL	94		IB
16	br	RS	45	tl	JT	60	tr	CM	95		JMN
20		WP/JB	46	tl/br	GM	61		DO	99		DO
24	tr/bl	SL	47	br	GM	66	b	KK	100–101		JT
26–27		SL	47	tl	IF	68	bl	DO	103		WP/JB
28		JT	48	tl	GM	68	tr	EF	105	tr	WP/JB
29	br	CM	48	br	CB	71		GI	106–107		GM
31	tr	MM	49	tl	GM	72–73		DO	108		JT
32		WP/JB	49	br	WP	75		SIL/LH	111		JT
34	br	CB	50	tl/br	GM	76	bl	SIL/WK	112		GM
34	bl	JMN	51	tl	IF	77		JT	114		JT
35	br	JT	51	br	GM	78	tr	GI	115		DO
38		DO	52	tl/br	GM	78	bl	CM	118		GI
39		DO	53	tl	GM	79		MM	119		JT
40–41		WP/KT	53	br	AL/JPF	82		DO	120		EF

Key to photographers: AL = Ardea London (JDM = Johan De Meester; JPF = JP Ferrero); CB = Carol Beuchat;
CM = Christelle Marais; DO = Dorothée von der Osten; EF = Elsa Flint; GI = Gallo Images; GM = Graham Meadows;
IB = Image Bank; IF = Isabelle Francais; JMN = Jade Maxwell Newton; JT = Johann Theron; KK = Karla Kik; MM = Melany
McCallum; RS = Robyn Steele; SIL = Struik Image Library (LH = Lanz von Hörsten; WK = Walter Knirr); SL = Simon Lewis;
WP = Warren Photographic (JB = Jane Burton; KT = Kim Taylor).
Key to locations: tl = top left; tr = top right; b = bottom, bl = bottom left; br = bottom right. (No abbreviation is given for
pages with a single image, or pages on which all photographs are by the same photographer.)